A STRING OF PAPER SUNS

AN EXPERIMENTAL MEMOIR

A String of Paper Suns: An Experimental Memoir

basiljander@gmail.com

ISBN: 978-0-578-44694-3

Cover design by: Fajar Wahyu S.B.
GoodMorningAfternoon by Kevin Christopher // KC Fonts

First Paperback Edition: January 2019

For Imani

AN EXPERIMENTAL MEMOIR

BRIDGET SILJANDER

Foreword

This book reflects my recollections and impressions of experiences over a period of time. All names, except Bridget and Imani, have been changed, some events have been compressed, and dialogue and details have been recreated. Most of the scenes describe actual events while a few are reimagined to capture the essence of aspects of my life.

Content note: This book's topics include trauma, crime, abuse, violence, domestic violence, sexual abuse and assault, rape, incest, child abuse, childhood sexual abuse and assault, abortion, critique of religion, mental health, suicide, disability, substance abuse, toxic relationships, sexual expression, poverty, and systemic oppression. This is not a comprehensive list. Reader discretion is advised.

Language note: In the disability community, there are different preferences around language: person-first vs. identity-first language. This is only one example. Person-first language emphasizes the person before the disability, for example, person with a disability. Identity-first language considers the disability to be part of the whole person, for example, disabled person. Generally, it is best practice to use a person's preferred language, which I have done in this book.

Table of Contents

Chapter 1: Giving Birth to Myself

"I think she's hemorrhaging. We need to get this baby out right now!" the doctor yelled. The hospital room filled with a team of medical professionals, rushing about, communicating frantically with each other in words that melted together in my morphine-saturated head as I convulsed in dulled pain off the bed. It was as if I were floating away into a peaceful state through the sound waves of their voices as they transferred my resigned teenaged body onto another bed for transport to the operating room.

As they continued to chatter while they whisked me through the hospital hallways, I looked groggily over at my panicked mother embracing my roommate, Jessica. "I will be fine," I said reassuringly as I flew away from them.

Whether or not I would actually be fine, I didn't know. All I could think about was saving my baby. I had to live and protect her from what had happened to me. Already, this fresh life was my purpose.

As a mask was placed on my face, I could feel my belly being prepared for emergency surgery. And then I was out cold.

* * *

A few hours later, when the anesthesia started to wear off, I lifted my heavy eyelids. Jessica smiled sweetly at me and gave me the news: "You have a beautiful little girl." She was here. I had a real baby. I fell back to sleep.

* * *

When the nurse checked on me, I asked about the nameless baby I had delivered in the night. I had been anticipating a son, who would be Demetrius—the name of a character in "A Midsummer Night's Dream"—the first play I had ever seen in a theater, just the year before. The nurse told me that my daughter was in the Neonatal Intensive Care Unit (NICU).

I ached to see what she looked like, this part of me. Her existence fascinated me—a new, tiny human. Somehow, I hoped that becoming a mother would erase everything that had transpired—that it would let me hit a reset button on my life. It began with a cute guy—someone who had good social skills and lots of self-confidence, qualities that I lacked. Maybe the combination of our DNA would create a better version of myself. Then I could live vicariously through my child, who would surely be the best parts of both parents—the way that blue and red make purple. I'd had an abortion a year earlier—this one, I had decided to keep. When I saw the ultrasound pictures of her and felt her flutter and kick, I couldn't wait to meet her. She was a promise of a better future.

Weak and reeling from the shock of unexpectedly having my pregnancy cut short and my baby taken abruptly from my womb, I climbed into a wheelchair and adjusted my hospital gown. My hair was a mess, but I had no vanity left at this point. As I was going to bed a few nights before, after a long day of working with an autistic child and a quadriplegic man, I had gone into labor, three months ahead of schedule. Jessica had driven me to the hospital as my contractions and bleeding increased, and I wept into my hands. When we pulled up to the emergency room, I looked at its doors—a tear-soaked, shattered nineteen year old with a growing dread that I was a failure—not only on my own behalf, but my innocent child's. I racked my brain trying to think of anything I could have done to trigger the labor. *Was it the two or three cigarettes I smoked a day during the past month or so? Should I not have been lifting disabled people at work? Had I accidentally drunk beer early on, before I knew I was pregnant? Could it have been the chlamydia I had gotten from a hookup a few weeks earlier? Or was it just that I wasn't supposed to be pregnant so young?*

Jessica pushed me now, down the hall toward the NICU, in anticipation of a grand introduction. We were buzzed into the department and approached the sign-in desk, where Joan, the receptionist, sat with a friendly smile and kind words. I was told about procedures and instructed to wash my hands for three minutes up to the elbows at a big sink with faucets you operated with your knees. I washed my hands and arms really well. This baby was going to have the best mom—a champion on her side always. I would not let her down!

I stood at the entrance of the nurseries filled with equipment and Isolettes. Machines hummed as medical students did their rounds, led by neonatologists, who explained the issues of these babies and their statuses. Some babies would cling to life, and some were too small and sick to make it. A nurse led me to the incubator with the label "Baby Girl Siljander." Inside I could see her delicate, dark, jaundiced body connected to life support. My eyes filled with tears, which wouldn't stop flowing. "I am your mother, little girl," I whispered. "I love you so much, and you are going to have a great life, I promise." She would have everything I didn't: freedom and the potential to be what she wanted to be. I would raise her to grow in self-love, instead of self-loathing.

I would name her Imani. It means faith.

Chapter 2: You Are My Sunshine

Sweetly and softly I sing, gazing out the living room window of a small three-bedroom home in an urban neighborhood in Phoenix. The street outside is iridescent from the desert heat. And the grass is parched: crispy and brown. A thirsty palm tree rises up in the far left corner of the lot. Its leaves are still. Sweat rolls down the back of my neck, soaking my striped T-shirt.

I stop singing for a moment to look down at the sleeping baby resting on my chest. Smiling, I gently stroke the baby's soft, velvety pink cheek. I take a deep breath as the baby coos. Smiling again as the baby's eyes flutter, I wonder what babies dream about. Dreams, how intriguing they are. We all have them. From the time we are babies. As I ponder the meaning of dreams, the baby becomes absolutely silent, except for the almost indistinguishable breath through his tiny nose.

Slowly and gracefully, I rock back and forth in my child-sized rocking chair—which had been my mother's—singing another song to my little brother Ryan, who is my third younger sibling. I am five years old. Ryan's wispy blond hair flutters with the movement. His content face is at peace with the world. In the arms of his older but young sister, he is protected and loved. Together, brother and sister are a cocoon of dreams. As much as I love my brother and other siblings, though, I dream for so many other things: uninterrupted playtime, enjoying books and friendships without distraction, and more attention from my parents.

Time stands still, as still as the palm leaves, the hot desert air. I kiss Ryan's buttery-soft cheek while he lays across me, arms limp without care around my sides.

We live near the Buttes, along the Cross Cut Canal near Griffith Elementary School and Pierce Park and a 7-Eleven. Our house has a fenced-in backyard and a carport. There are brown and beige cement planters in the front of the house and on the patio in the back. Our grass is always hard and loaded with pickers that stick to our feet. We run around barefoot anyway. We have neighbors on each side: an older couple—a woman and a man who is always drunk and calling for his dog "Booger"—and a family that often has rowdy visitors on the other. The fence at the back edge of our yard is cement brick with a big, dark wooden gate that is always locked so we won't get out and fall in the canal just beyond...

Our one-level home is warm and happy, like a chocolate chip cookie right out of the oven. In the living room are dark brown wood panels lining the walls and multi-tonal brown shag carpet. The kitchen in the back of the house has speckled vinyl flooring, and there is a wooden kitchen table in front of the sliding glass door to the patio, where a plant with long vines hangs. In the bathroom is busy floral wallpaper and a yellow bathtub. It has a door into my parents' room and one into the hallway, which leads to the other two bedrooms—one for the boys and one for the girls.

Mom is pretty, thin, and has a feathered hairstyle like Farrah Fawcett. She wears perfume for church on Sundays and smokes cigarettes like a fashion model. Dad is thin, too, and has shaggy dark brown hair like The Beatles wore. He smokes cigarettes like a rock star.

They are trendy for congregants of the Laestadian Lutheran Church, which frowns upon following the latest styles.

There are conveniently placed ashtrays in the house and extras when "company" visit us—usually after church on Sundays. Smoking is the only vice allowed by the church.

Drinking, dancing, movies, television, friends outside of church, makeup and earrings, listening to anything other than church and classical music, organized sports, extracurricular activities, and most forms of entertainment are strictly prohibited.

We keep to a select circle and often listen to church music or sing together when we socialize. Sometimes my dad plays folk music on the guitar and I sing. We record ourselves using a magnetic tape recorder. I like hearing my voice played back to me because Dad says it is beautiful.

During music class at school, teachers roll in a music cart with a record player and a stack of records. We sing a lot of favorites like "Goober Peas," "It Ain't Gonna Rain No More," "This Old Man (Knick-Knack Patty-Whack)," "Take Me Out to the Ball Game," and "Old Dan Tucker." And we learn subjects, like math, by listening to records.

Five time three is fif-TEEN and five times four is TWEN-ty!

Five times five is twenty-FIVE, and five times six is THIR-ty!

I get so excited seeing the cart roll into the classroom, hearing the sound of the needle dropping with a scratching sound on the record. I love memorizing all the songs, so I can sing them over and over, my voice clear and bright.

As I sing, I imagine God up in Heaven, angry that I am not being good enough, and that I never can be. If I want to wear nail polish—to see what it's like—or talk to a friend outside the church too much, I am having "temptations." "He" is always mad and ready to condemn us to damnation. Maybe if I just sing more and more, I'll be saved and He won't condemn my friends either.

"Are you ready to sing 'You Are My Sunshine,' little Bridgie?" Dad asks with a kind smile as he comes in from the back yard where he was assembling a swing set. He trades me a microphone for baby Ryan and puts him in his car seat next to me.

"Yes, Daddy, I'm ready to sing; I know the words," I say with exuberance. Picking up his guitar and sliding the pick out of the neck, he begins to strum. I know exactly when to come in…

I sing to my baby brother, Ryan, as I watch his sleeping face begin to stir.

Chapter 3: Changing Tunes and Diapers

I stood gazing at Imani from above the top of the protective face mask, feeling my hot breath against my face. Her features were miniature like a porcelain doll I had gotten from my parents for Christmas, to match one my grandmother had in her collection. Looking around at the area surrounding the Isolette, I noted all the things Imani needed: a temperature-controlled, clean (and sometimes sterile) environment, hair-thin tubing, blood pressure cuffs the size of Band-Aids, and sensitive equipment that measured the slightest changes in vital signs. There were all the proportionate items that fit her, like diapers as small as a credit card and socks that looked like they could fit over the tip of your finger. Her thin, translucent skin was not fully developed, so she couldn't wear clothes yet. Her body was not ready to live outside of me.

I would be resilient and accepting of whatever I was told. My background had prepared me for this—but beyond that, I loved her so much that I would do anything for her. She was my child, my whole world now.

"Are you Mom?" the nurse asked me. That startled me a bit.

"Yes, I am Mom," I managed, as I attempted to own the words.

Observing my two-pound, six-ounce baby through the thick plastic of her environment-controlled Isolette, I listened as the nurse recited a long list of my daughter's very serious problems.

Because of the trauma of delivery and my baby's weak blood vessels, she had a brain hemorrhage. Blood had filled the ventricles, pushing the tissue toward her skull, threatening to crush it under the pressure. The fluid overflowed, pooling, pulling the skin with it, so it lay next to her head like a flat bubble. While I had been in labor, I was given steroid shots to strengthen the blood vessels in her brain, as well as her lungs. They had gone into effect mere hours before delivery.

She was on a ventilator because she couldn't breathe on her own.

She had severe jaundice.

She was on an IV, which went into her head that delivered fluids and nutrition.

It would not be known for months if she would be able to see, or if she would be blind, due to a condition called "retinopathy of prematurity."

For the first several days, I stood watch by my baby's Isolette, enthralled with everything she did. I spoke in a hushed voice because she was so fragile, just to let her know that I was there. Her hands waved around like she was doing an interpretive dance to music that only she could hear. Then her arms and hands stiffened and punched the air as her body writhed and she cried, in silence. It broke my heart that the ventilator down her throat robbed her of her voice. I put my hand on the Isolette, which was as close as I could get to touching her, to provide comfort.

"Bridget! Did you notice how special your little angel looks today?" her nurse, Karen, exclaimed on day three, coming behind me. Drawing closer to the Isolette, I peered in at my tiny baby attached to tubes and sensors under three banks of lights. Her miniature face was covered with an eye guard attached to pieces of Velcro stuck to the sides of her head. And on top of her soft head, still recovering from birth trauma, adorned by a sparse coat of jet-black hair, was a bright pink bow, set in K-Y Jelly.

"You can put your hand on her back soon," Karen told me, "but only for a little bit because preemies get over-stimulated quickly." She gave me a hug, which she did every time she saw me. It made me feel warm all over, and safe—like everything would be OK because she was there. I needed her validation after having been abandoned during my pregnancy, and before that, losing everything. Here in this NICU on the University of Minnesota campus, I was more than a teen mom, and my daughter was more than my assumed mistake. We were important. I hugged Karen again.

Karen had a heart-shaped face and a heart-shaped life. Close to retirement, she was still as joyous as someone just beginning a career of her dreams. Her smile shone from her eyes as she worked.

"OK, honey, I need to change the angel's diaper," Karen reminded herself cheerfully. Singing a tune without words in her melodic voice, she opened both of the oval doors to the Isolette by pushing the latches and put one arm in each side. Turning my baby slightly, she slid a fresh diaper under her, underneath the dirty diaper, which she tucked under her. Then she turned her the other way, pulling the fresh diaper through and pulling the dirty diaper out. Since Imani's skin was sensitive, she did not tape the diaper but left it open with my baby lying on top of it.

I watched and tried to learn as much as I could. Even though I had taken care of my many siblings and children in my church and neighborhood, this was new, ever-changing territory. I thought of what my grandmother had always told me: "No soul will be lost."

* * *

A week after Imani was born, I came home from a long day at the hospital to find Jessica chain-smoking cigarettes and doing her acrylic nails. Our intimate studio apartment in Uptown Minneapolis—in a charming old building that some claimed was haunted—was filled with noxious fumes and a thick haze that hung low. Jessica, who I had met through a co-worker, had moved in with me the previous summer and had treated me to big meals fit for a pregnant mom-to-be. I'd tolerated her activities then, even participated in one or two, but times had changed.

"Hey, Jess, I would feel better if you could go out of the apartment to smoke or do your nails. I'm pumping my breast milk, and the fumes and smoke can go into my milk. Plus I think that we should start getting ready for Imani at the apartment. She's going to be weaker than a typical baby, and healthy babies can't be around that stuff anyway."

Jessica looked at me incredulously with lowered eyes and said, "I live here, too, so don't start being a bitch again."

"I wasn't being a bitch," I replied immediately, tensing. "When YOU didn't pay YOUR rent, you stressed me out and it triggered my labor." My fondness for my occasionally nurturing but erratic friend slipped away just like that. I had a baby to protect now.

"Well, you didn't have to go off on me," Jessica snapped, "so you don't deserve an apology."

"Oh really?! I don't deserve an apology when my baby is two pounds and in the NICU?!" My heart started pounding, and my motherhood instincts kicked in like a mama bear's. Her ability to be so flippant when my baby was struggling to survive was unconscionable and pissed me right off.

"Just shut the fuck up," Jessica retaliated, standing up and changing the CD in her stereo. For the rest of the evening, she blasted Madonna and fumed up our apartment with her nails and smoking. Livid but without recourse, I dumped the next two batches of breast milk because I was sure they were contaminated.

Unable to sleep and with racing thoughts, I went back to the hospital to be with my baby. *How in the hell am I going to make a home for my baby with Jessica's diva and dangerous antics and no support system?*

Karen had gone home, and a nurse I had not yet met was on duty. We said hello and introduced ourselves. I sat in a rocking chair next to the Isolette and rocked myself slowly, pushing my feet sleepily off the floor, as I peered at my baby in the dim light.

The situation at home with Jessica was unacceptable. There was no way I was going to tolerate the smoking, acrylic nail fumes, yelling, stress, or disharmony. Imani needed to go home to a place that was healthy and happy with people who loved her and took good care of her.

For now, my baby was surviving, and so was I. And as I spoke to her gently through the box, her vital signs became rhythmic on the machines above. She knew that I was there.

* * *

A couple weeks later, Imani was growing well and had recovered the weight she had lost after her birth—back to two and a half pounds. Jessica still wasn't working and spent her time dying her hair blonder and perfecting her French tip acrylic nails, in between chain smoking. She had started seeing AJ, her high school sweetheart, again. He was almost as blonde as she was, worked construction, had a muscular physique, and drove a pickup truck. She finished her cigarette and we drove together to the hospital.

As I drove, Jessica, beaming with the sparkle of a rekindled love, chirped, "Bridge, how has Imani been doing?"

"She went back on the ventilator after they tried the CPAP machine, but otherwise, she's doing good," I informed her.

"Oh wow, she is such a princess! I just love her little face and those LIPS!" Jessica shrieked. "Her lips will be so pouty-perfect when that ventilator finally comes out."

Jessica talked about Imani as though she were a young girl opening a present and discovering that it was the doll she had wanted.

"Karen—you know, the nurse—said that she might get it out today. But it depends on if she's breathing above the vent enough—like breathing more than the machine," I explained.

Jessica was giggling about something that AJ had done on their date the night before as we went up in the elevator. We entered the same double doors that I went through every day—usually multiple times a day. Joan wasn't there because it was the weekend, and instead, the weekend receptionist asked us to sign in and make sure to note the patient's name.

As we washed our hands and arms in the sinks outside the rooms, Jessica continued bubbling about AJ. "Oh, Bridge! He is so hot, and we're going to have the cutest little towhead kids. I want three. At least one girl so I can dress her up like a princess. You'll be her godmother, and our girls will play together and be best friends."

Jessica's plans made me feel like everything would even out for me within a couple years, compared to everyone else my age. I wouldn't have the stigma anymore of a teenaged, unwed mother. "Out of wedlock," the church whispered about me.

Jessica handed me a paper towel because the dispenser on my side was out. As I dried my hands, I looked at photos and stories posted to a bulletin board: children that had been in the NICU who were now toddlers, school age, and teenagers. My eyes moistened, and my heart filled with hope. I imagined that Imani would grow up and leave this place and have a happy life. We went into the NICU and noticed that the curtain was pulled around Imani. I looked at Jessica with slight concern, and her face sobered. We stood outside the curtain and waited.

A nurse walked up behind us and said that the curtain was closed because Imani was having a lot of "spells"—or "forgetting" to breathe, so her vital signs dropped—and she needed less stimulation. The NICU could be very noisy and busy with all of the medical staff—doctors, nurses, therapists, specialists, students, etc.—and family—parents, siblings, grandparents, aunts, uncles, cousins, other family, and friends.

I asked if we could still see her.

"Sure," she said, "but just be quiet and try not to disturb her."

Jessica and I took turns sitting in the rocking chair by the Isolette, not saying anything. We watched Imani and shared looks with each other that communicated our reactions to her—I raised my eyebrows in alarm, glancing at the Isolette and back at Jessica to see what she thought, and Jessica bit her lower lip with a pained expression of empathy.

Imani was motionless, except for an occasional hand gesture or leg stretch, and silent on the ventilator. She was down to two banks of lights for jaundice and still wore the eye guard. Her IV remained in her head to provide her with nutrition, hydration, and medication.

It was like she knew we were there, and she relaxed; her heart rate, blood pressure, and breathing stabilized. Through the plastic of the Isolette, I whispered, "I love you, baby." Inside the shroud of the curtain, it hit me that Imani's life was precarious. I dreamed of her emancipation, of creating a future for her that was magnificent. A witch who lived in my apartment building had done a tarot reading and told me that Imani and I both would be victorious. She also gathered a group of her friends and we sat in a circle to do a Wiccan healing water ritual in the party room. Many people loved Imani already.

I imagined her growing and blossoming into a child with a personality and wondered if she would be much like me when I was young: sweet, shy, curious, studious, and eager to please. Or would she be what I wished I could have been if I had grown up outside the confines of the church? I hoped for the latter—a self-assured, more whole, less damaged version of myself.

Chapter 4: Windows to the World

Perched, angling for a view of the storybook pages, we kids forge positions on the couch, challenging its capacity, to hear our mother read a book to us. Mom has a voice for each character, which matches their vibes, and she adds a theatrical flair. Every week, we pile into our Ford station wagon and head to the library. We fill our arms with books about everything, books with cassette tapes, and books with pictures. I keep a stash in my room at all times.

"Which book should I read first?" Mom asks us with outward anticipation. I have The Fox Went Out on a Chilly Night, Ottie and the Star, *and* Where the Wild Things Are.

"I want Dr. Suess!" my younger brother Sam proclaims. He is four years old and trying to learn how to read. I have been teaching him some words.

"I read him One Fish, Two Fish, Red Fish, Blue Fish, *and he liked it," I say.*

Mom agrees to start with that. Then voting will commence again.

As usual, we insist that she read all the books in the latest stack from the library.

"Who wants to look at the stars before bed, like Ottie did?" Mom asks.

A cheer of "I do! I do! I do!" erupts, and we follow Mom outside to our backyard patio.

It is dark outside, and there are a lot of stars for being so close to the city. I hold my stuffed animals—pink and blue rabbits with rattles inside, which I had gotten from my grandparents—and point them so they can also look at the stars with us.

"Mom, where is heaven?" I ask.

"It's past the stars."

"Can we see it?"

"No, but we believe in it because God tells us so."

"How do we know that God is real?"

"We read the Bible, and it tells us about God."

"So the Bible is real?"

"Yes, the Bible is God's word."

"Can God see what I'm doing right now?"

"God sees everything, and He sees us right now."

"I'm scared of God."

"We don't have to be scared of God because He loves us."

"But He's always watching us to see if we are being bad."

"If we try not to sin and get our sins forgiven, then we do not have to be afraid."

"What if I don't always know if I'm sinning and it makes God angry?"

"Do you want your sins forgiven to make sure you don't have sins on your conscience?"

"Yes, please forgive my sins," I plead. "And trespassings; I learned that in Sunday School."

"Believe all your sins forgiven in Jesus' name and precious blood."

When my mom says those words, I feel relieved that I am once again redeemed in the eyes of God and that I will not be marked for Hell. It makes me want to ask for my sins to be forgiven as often as possible because I do not know when something I did might be a sin. In Sunday School, I learned that having doubts was a sin. What was a doubt? Was it OK to think about what the Bible said or what the ministers preached? Was it a sin to care about people outside of the church, even though they were "unbelievers?"

What if I died before getting my sins forgiven? God is hard to understand. Questioning what I am told is a sin. It seems like everything is a sin! When I saw a girl at school kiss a boy, I worried that she was going to Hell, but I was too shy to tell her to get her sins forgiven. "Please, God," I pray to myself, "don't let her die with sin on her conscience; her parents are unbelievers and didn't tell her it was bad."

"Mom, can you forgive my sins again before I go to bed?"

"You can ask me whenever you want."

"Thank you, Mom." I don't think that my mom or dad ever sin.

Chapter 5: Community Sister

On three hours of sleep, after staying at the hospital until 5:00 a.m. and getting up at 8:30 a.m. for my job as a caregiver, I drank most of a pot of coffee and smoked two cigarettes. After two weeks of recovering from my emergency Cesarean section, I had returned to work because I didn't have any savings or paid time off. My first shift of the day was one I had picked up to help an elderly woman get ready and eat breakfast before a doctor appointment. Then there was a break for a few hours before my next shift, so I went home to have lunch, pump breast milk, and nap.

There was a pause after a stream of kids got off the school bus in south Minneapolis. Then I saw Cole, who was eleven years old, moving intentionally down the bus steps. He was smiling and staring blankly, with his shock of blonde hair blowing in the crisp fall breeze. His empty-looking backpack was partway open, but there was nothing at risk of falling out. Without making eye contact, he made a bee-line for the front door, which was open, and barged into the kitchen.

On the counter, he found string cheese and peanut butter crackers that I had prepared for him moments before. As if he hadn't eaten all day, he scarfed them down and then asked, "Milk?"

"Oh, sorry, Cole, I will get you a glass of milk."

"Milk!" he said, raising his voice.

"One minute, Cole," I reassured him, opening the refrigerator door and pulling out the carton of milk—then grabbed a glass from the clean dishwasher, even though it wasn't dry.

Before I finished pouring the glass of milk, he plunked himself in front of the television on his favorite chair, and found *The Simpsons*. Stomping his feet, he laughed and pointed. "Homer silly!"

We shared a chuckle. Then I asked, "Do you want your milk now?"

"Yes!" he replied, taking the glass and drinking it down.

When the episode was over, I asked him if he wanted to do some stretching exercises, and he agreed, picking up a toy truck he liked to play with. First, we took off his leg braces, and he sat on the floor. Starting with his calf muscles, I held his left knee and pushed his foot toward him, then did his right side. In ten minutes, I stretched his calves, hamstrings, quadriceps, and hip flexors, to keep him limber because cerebral palsy causes muscle spasticity.

Cole, who was also intellectually disabled and autistic, needed constant supervision and support because he was vulnerable and unsafe if left alone. I had been working with him more since my college semester ended; I hadn't registered for another one because I was pregnant.

Sometimes he got very anxious and overwhelmed, so he would hit and throw things. He had hit me once in my pregnant belly when he wasn't able to regulate his emotions. He didn't want to feel like that and couldn't help it. I understood. When my anxiety spiked, I couldn't think straight because my head felt like a balloon that had been blown up too much. When I was pissed about a grade, I'd kick my car tires and tell them to fuck off. I screamed at my parents when I got sick of them controlling me and threw things, like my backpack. Once I hurled a vacuum cleaner at the wall, since I couldn't untangle the cord and was already having a bad day. These outbursts happened as I got older and went through puberty. Younger me only cried or stopped talking or hid somewhere. After Cole got his feelings out, he was smiling and vocalizing again—and rocking more rhythmically instead of jerking hard.

After stretching, Cole liked to relax with video games. That was when I went to the bathroom to pump my breast milk for Imani and put it into small, plastic, labeled cups. A lactation consultant had trained me and provided the machine that came with bottles attached to suction cups. It took me about ten minutes if I turned the machine on high. Cole's sister, Ricky, who was fourteen years old, sat with him while I was gone, but I still hurried.

My breasts were tender as I turned off the suction and pulled the cups off. Every two hours, around the clock, pumping had to be done to produce enough milk and not dry up.

"Ricky, you can go in a minute. I'm just about done," I yelled down the stairs, peeking out of the dirty bathroom, which looked like it hadn't been cleaned in months. Ricky didn't say anything. It was hard to know what she was thinking, and she didn't share.

On my way back down the stairs, I was met by Cole's mother, Beate, who practically cornered me. "Marriage is hard enough without a disabled child," she hissed. Stunned, I had no time to react, just looked at her with big eyes that conveyed no understanding of what she meant. My heart started to pound as I slowly distanced myself from her and tried to avoid her husband so I wouldn't add fuel to her jealousy. When her husband made conversation with me, she would yell at him to be a better husband and pay more attention to her.

I returned to Cole, who was shrieking in the living room, so I could get him ready for his bath. He hated taking a bath, so he usually fought me to get into the tub, splashing water everywhere and knocking bottles off the bathroom shelves.

By this time, it was already a full day. Working split shifts—two hours here and four hours there—my days were extremely long with big, unpaid gaps in between shifts when I was commuting back and forth and unable to do anything productive. I was also too tired to. My paycheck was $270 a week after taxes, and I was also supporting Jessica so she could babysit Imani.

Next stop was Mark, who also lived in South Minneapolis. Mark broke his neck in a football accident when he was in high school. He told me the correct term was "spinal cord injury." But he still went on to go to college. He didn't like when I cracked my neck—something I did habitually to calm myself—because it reminded him of his injury. Mark told me that one of his doctors early on suggested that he learn everything about his body after his injury so that he could teach other people how to assist him. He walked me through everything that I needed to do. During my pregnancy he would criticize how people treated me, saying I deserved better. A lot of the time, he was the only one person who was nice to me.

Mark's front door was open when I arrived at his charming old home with hardwood flooring and walls adorned with photos of him and his friends like his Berkeley college buddies, known as the "Rolling Quads," a group of wheelchair users who identified with their disabilities and challenged the notion that disabled people couldn't go to college and have careers.

"Come in!" Mark hollered from his office at the front of the house, where he ran his motivational speaking business. He spoke at schools throughout the year, and I remembered him speaking at my middle school some years before. He brought "Bones," a small skeleton that he used to demonstrate how the spinal cord works. He told our class "The problem isn't the issue; the issue is how you deal with the problem." That made me realize that life was about perspective, something I was trying hard to remember. The slogan of Mark's company was: "What he has to say may change your life."

"I'm not ready yet; I'm trying to finish an email," he said impatiently. I sat on a chair in his living room and looked around at his antique wooden folding cameras with lenses that extended from a box. My dad had four such cameras on bookshelves in our living room. I couldn't remember the last time I spoke to my parents.

"I'll get your room ready and clean up. No rush."

"Yeah. It's really pissing me off that this school had me speak at their pep rally last year and now they won't even return my calls for this year. I can't keep waiting around. I have to pay my MA spend-down to keep my PCA services."

"Dang, that sucks, Mark. What's an MA spend-down?"

Swinging around in his power wheelchair, he faced me, his arm splint still on his right arm. His flashing eyes were bright blue and indignant and almost looked like they were mocking me for not understanding his plight.

He explained that an MA spend-down is a monthly payment that you have to make to subsidize your Medical Assistance or Medicaid—a government program that provides health care and other services.

"You have to be poor enough to qualify for MA and your spend-down is based on your income if you make above a certain number," he continued in his teacher voice.

"Uh huh," I said, trying to follow.

"My business pays me a percentage of what it grosses, or pays before taxes. So I need enough to pay my spend-down, but not too much—in order to stay on MA." It sounded like a dilemma.

I sighed sympathetically and shifted in my chair. His eyes conveyed his determination to make his message clear for his neophyte audience of one.

Raising his voice slightly with emphasis, he repeated what he said to present it in another way. "I need MA. It pays for my healthcare and that includes you. I can't get out of bed in the morning without a PCA."

Blinking at Mark, I waited for him to say something that made sense to me.

"Ha!" He laughed. "You're still a teenager. Hopefully you won't have to learn about this BS anytime soon… Before I forget, my mom brought some crib sheets and clothes for Imani, and the bag is on the bench by the front door."

We went into Mark's bedroom, which was connected to his bathroom. To the right was a waterbed with a headboard full of medical and adaptive equipment and supplies, plus a tape recorder, which he used to play hypnosis tapes that helped him sleep. At the foot of the bed was a standing frame. He stood in it to bear weight on his bones to make them stronger and to improve his circulation and avoid pressure sores from sitting too long. To the left of that was a shelf with his nighttime leg braces. And to the left of his bed was an antique dresser with a mirror, with his medications and miscellaneous medical supplies on the top. Every week, I refilled his pillbox for AM and PM for each day of the week. Next to his pillbox, he kept a small water pitcher from the hospital with a handle and a flexible straw in it.

Since his water pitcher still had some water in it, he asked me to give it to him. I slipped it over his hand, resting the hook of the handle in the cradle between his thumb and pointer finger. It was sort of like bobbing for apples to get ahold of the straw, but he had practiced for decades. After he took a slurp, I poured the pills from the appropriate day of the week into his curled hand for him to swallow.

Bedtime was very routine, and I knew all the steps that Mark wanted carried out. Usually he wore a button-down dress shirt and V-neck sweater. I would pull the sweater over his head, then unbutton his shirt, pulling it off one arm at a time. After unrolling the sleeves (he liked them rolled up twice to his elbows), I tossed them into a laundry basket. He brushed his teeth next with a towel on his chest over his corset (abdominal binder), using a toothbrush attached to a splint, which slipped over his hand the same way the pitcher did. I drenched a washcloth in hot water, wrung it out, and placed it on his face for a few seconds before he leaned forward to drop it into his hand and wipe his face.

Transferring Mark into bed was the hardest but fastest part of the night. From the bathroom, he backed into his bedroom and parallel parked next to his waterbed. Then he shut off the power on his wheelchair. First, I pulled his butt forward in the seat by pulling on his knees from underneath—which was followed by hugging his upper body under his arms and grabbing the top of his pants in back. Once my legs were in position, bracing his knees, I partially stood him up and rotated him toward his bed to sit him down. He sank into his waterbed gently, and I put him down slowly and swung his legs over the bed. Sometimes I had to hoist him up a little higher in the bed and straighten him out, since transfers were more about making the mark and less about the details.

"Bridget, I need you to set my alarm for 6:00 a.m.; I have a doctor appointment at 10:00 a.m." Even with an abbreviated morning, it would still take us three hours to get through the routine. You can get in with the key under the mailbox."

"Alright, well, I'm going to wrap this up since it's almost midnight and we both have an early morning. Let me just get your leg braces and CPAP machine on, and we can call it a night."

"Yep."

Hennepin Avenue was peaceful as I drove home. The sidewalks were dotted with people, including a trickle of well-to-do folks leaving Figlio's. What I wouldn't give for a fun night out. Someone was in my parking spot again, so I had to park on the street five blocks down and walk home in the dark by myself. I yawned all the way home with my purse slung wearily over my shoulder. "Hey girl," a drunk man slurred, waving at me limply from across the street. Clutching my purse in front of me, I quickened my pace to get home to my baby.

Chapter 6: Say What?

Carrying my My Little Pony tin lunch box, I arrive at school. Griffith Elementary has an open campus with rows of classrooms that form a rectangle. Hallways line the interior perimeter, and there is a courtyard in the center.

Our principal is a slender, silver-haired woman who always wears red lipstick. I don't know how old she is, but she seems grown up and is the epitome of a career woman.

Careful not to step on cracks in the sidewalk (I avoid them obsessively), I walk across the playground toward the swings, where I usually play alone during recess.

One kid hollers, "Hey, girl, why don't you talk so we can hear what your voice sounds like?!"

After stopping to pause, I ask meekly, "What do you want me to say?" and keep walking before waiting for a response.

Once in my classroom, I slide into my desk and pull out a Nancy Drew Mystery book. It is exciting to read about the exploits of Nancy Drew and her friends—young women who solve mysteries. Literature shows me how big the world is.

Behind me, two girls sit down and start talking about Garbage Pail Kids and trading cards. I want to join them, but I feel like there is a gate inside me that won't let my voice out. Besides, they are a year older than me, since I have just skipped a grade and today is my first day in second grade.

My parents wave proudly to me from my new classroom window, and I lift my head slightly to acknowledge them. Mrs. French continues with her lesson as if nothing had happened as I try to blend in and do what I think I am supposed to do.

A girl sitting next to me points to where we are in the workbook. A couple of other kids whisper as they look at me, and I feel my face reddening—hoping that I won't be noticed for plopping into the class. I don't think I am smart or "gifted," as I am now labeled. I just want to learn in my own way.

It is strange and upsetting, but I don't have the words for my feelings. And trying to interpret other people is confusing, like listening to a radio in between two stations.

When recess is over that afternoon, I walk toward where the kids are lining up, looking at the ground. Ms. Lopez asks me what is wrong.

"I don't have any friends," I whisper.

"Come here. Let's help you make some friends," she says gently.

"Class, can I get your attention, please? Who would like to be Bridget's friends?"

There is silence except for a few feet shuffling. Then Aisha from my class comes forward and says, "I will be your friend, Bridget." I look up at her with gratitude and walk with her to the back of the line.

During class, Ms. Lopez describes what it is like to have multiple sclerosis as she hands out MS Read-a-Thon pledge forms. We can't see her MS because it is a disability on the inside. I want to read as many books as I can to make MS go away because she said she can see two of everything and it makes her lose her balance. She is the prettiest, kindest, smartest teacher in the school. I want her to live a long time and love more kids like she loves me. Maybe one day I will learn to talk about my feelings like she talks about her MS.

Chapter 7: Circumstances

On a Wednesday morning before work, I met with Tricia, the hospital social worker, to see if she could help me make ends meet. A week before, I had already visited Hennepin County Human Services to apply for public assistance, but it was going to take a while before my application could go through.

"How are you feeling, Bridget?" Tricia asked, leaning toward me and looking me in the eyes.

Sighing, I responded with the hesitation of someone who was unsure and in flux but wanted to inspire confidence: "I'm…I'm getting everything set up for Imani to come home."

"Good for you," she assured me. "What else do you need for that to happen?"

Laughing uncomfortably, I over-explained, "I wasn't really expecting this and I was OK financially. I mean, not great, but I could pay my bills. My parents said that they would help me out but then told me to try going to the government. They don't even call anymore, and my mom said they don't visit because they don't like my 'unbeliever' roommate, and I have a new brother they need to take care of, too. I still haven't even paid my rent, and we're halfway through the month. My landlord said she would give me some time, and that helped me so I could get groceries and stuff. But I have no way of making it to the end of the month. My roommate doesn't always pay her part of the rent or other bills, and she eats my food. She has her own issues. It sucks asking for help, and it's embarrassing, but I'm scared."

"We all need help sometimes, and it's nothing to be ashamed of," Tricia comforted me. "And there is a charity that helps with rent in emergencies. I'll print the paperwork, and you can come back tomorrow to do that. Also, do you know about Social Security?"

"Oh gosh, OK, thank you, Tricia," I stammered. "I can come back tomorrow at the same time. What do you mean about Social Security?"

She explained that I could apply for Supplemental Security Income (SSI) through Social Security for Imani since she was disabled and expected to remain disabled, or die. And we were poor, so it would help with basic expenses like rent. If approved, she would also be eligible for Medical Assistance, for disabled and low-income people. I told her that I thought I could be on my parents' health insurance through my dad's job. That was fine, she confirmed, but she insisted it would be good to get Imani on MA, considering her medical issues and possible long-term needs. She told me if I didn't stay in college, I might not be able to remain on my dad's insurance and that Medicaid covered a lot of things that Imani might need that standard insurance wouldn't.

My hands started to shake, and the room got blurry. Tricia's words started to reverberate against each other in my head. Putting my hands on her desk, I leaned back and stood up, taking a long breath. She said the word: "disabled." Imani would qualify for programs I'd never even heard of because she was "disabled." It seemed like it was all my fault—that I was to blame that my child couldn't be on regular insurance, was going to be on all these programs, and felt like a ward of the State. What had I done to this beautiful baby?

"How am I going to do this?" I asked Tricia. Pacing her office, I blurted out, "I had no idea—no idea…I never anticipated any of this. When I found out that I was pregnant, I didn't think that my life would change." I felt guilty, and foolish, for not anticipating the potential consequences of my decision.

"It'll be fine!" Marcus insists. "I'm going to live up to my responsibilities. Growing up, I didn't have a father around, and I'm NOT going to do that to MY child."

I can see how resolved he is and how visceral his determination is to be in our child's life. I can do this. I can move forward with this pregnancy. We can be a family—a happy little family of our own. He has my heart, and I am in love.

"Bridget," Tricia said, putting her hand on my shoulder, "this happens to a lot of girls like you. Youth who don't have a strong support system are at-risk. I think it's also harder for you to read social cues and know when people are manipulating you."

Not sure what she meant, I didn't say anything. She continued, "With everything that has happened to you…"

"You don't think I'm a loser or a bad person? Almost everyone treats me like I'm stupid and says I brought this on myself," I told her. My coworker had shaken her head and wouldn't look at me when I told her I was pregnant and keeping the baby. I saw how people in public looked at me with my funky-colored hair, piercings, and baby bump. Their collective judgment burned a hole into me.

Tricia shook her head and said, "You're neither of those things. A lot of people don't understand; they don't see how circumstances in people's lives can lead to future situations. Many of them think that we have more control over our lives than we do. And that's not to say that you didn't make some choices that led to this, but your thinking was influenced by your experiences."

Sitting down again, on the edge of my chair, I sighed. "I wish everyone was as nice as you," I lamented. "I never thought I would be here…" Maybe she was right. I had been through a lot, but I was always told that I should "think positive," that other people had it harder than me. People didn't always know what they were talking about.

Tricia handed me her business card and said that she was happy to do what she could, and that I could call her. She told me that I wasn't alone and she would help me by connecting me with a support network in the community.

That afternoon, after my first shift and before my second, Marcus and I signed a "recognition of parentage" in the hospital, acknowledging that he was Imani's father, and talked about giving Imani his last name. Karen notarized it for us. He had pressured me into signing it, threatening to take me to court if I didn't, even though he was always saying that he didn't want to deal with the courts.

"You don't have money for a lawyer," he warned me. "And you know I'm the father, unless there's something you haven't told me. I know you were slutting around Minneapolis."

Frightened by his forceful command and ashamed that I was questioning whether he was the father, I nervously and submissively reassured him. "Marcus, no, no, no, you are the father! Can't you see that she looks like you?" Whenever I gazed at Imani, I loved her so much it ached, but sometimes,

I examined her hoping to see Marcus clearly reflected in her features.

He looked at me sideways and growled, "You better not be lying to me because you're putting me through a lot of drama for nothing if you are!" Our pact to be united parents for our child had long since evaporated. We were not the happy little family of three. Instead, we didn't trust each other and could barely communicate or cooperate—and Imani was in the middle of the turmoil.

The next day, I went back to Tricia's office with my proof of income and completed the application for emergency rent assistance and other hospital paperwork.

I completed all of the paperwork very carefully. There was no room for mistakes or delays because I needed help urgently and had no cushion.

After reviewing my paperwork several times, I handed it to Tricia. "I think I got everything."

"I'm sure you did, but I'll take a look at it," Tricia said. She flipped through the pages, underlining some of the parts with her finger. "Looks good," she confirmed, looking up at me with a pleased expression that conveyed assurance and validation of my efforts.

"Thank you, Tricia. I don't know what I would do without you—really, I don't," I said, almost pleading with her to not stop helping me.

Imani was approved for SSI. Her monthly payment was a whopping was $3.16. It was based on my income, which was below the poverty line.

Chapter 8: Before I Knew It Was Wrong

I want to be outside. It is a beautiful, hot desert day, and there is a grassy area behind the church to run and frolic. My vista is framed by church windows made of pale, overly polished wood with crosses in the middle. Daydreaming, I imagine picking the violet flowers near the curb of the parking lot, and then sitting in the grass to contemplate the petals.

Sometimes after church, I roll down the hill near the back entrance, watching the world spin as I let gravity take over, and momentum quickens the revolutions. Clouds, ground, clouds, ground… When I get to the bottom after about ten seconds, I run up to the top of the hill, lie down, and propel myself to initiate another circular plunge. Laughing when I get too close to a friend or almost collide with someone's feet. The minister adjusts his own microphone and then the minister's next to him.

"In the name of God, the Father, the Son, and the Holy Ghost, we ask you to bless our congregation. You are our creator, protector, and the One who will lead us to our heavenly home. We thank thee for thy grace, as we are sinful and weak…"

The prayer lasts for fifteen minutes, and is then translated into Finnish. Afterward, I lean over to talk to my Auntie Rose in her wheelchair and I tell her I like church, thinking that it is over. She gives me a pad of paper to write on to occupy me.

"Vuonna Jumalan nimissä, Isä, Poika ja Pyhä Henki, pyydämme sinua siunaamaan seurakunnassamme. Olet meidän luoja, suojelija, ja se, joka johtaa meidät taivaalliseen kotiimme. Kiitämme teitä."

We sit through an hour-long sermon about how we need to be childlike in our faith.

"Know ye not, that to whom ye yield yourselves servants to obey, his servants ye are to whom ye obey; whether of sin unto death, or of obedience unto righteousness."

I half-listen as I look around the sanctuary.

From the front row, I can see the faces of almost everyone. The adults are listening intently, or appear to be. They look from the minister to their children, making sure they are behaving.

When my friend Kate's mom isn't looking, she makes a face at her younger brother, Zach. He punches her, and Kate tattles to her mom. That is when Kate's mom takes Zach out of church for a time-out. Everyone turns and watches them proceed all the way down the aisle, to see what will happen. It is a distraction, momentary relief from the boredom.

When I check to see who else is gawking, I notice that my usually jovial grandfather is looking at me with disdain for not minding my own business. I was taught to respect my elders, so I redirect my attention to the sermon, even though I'm still not listening. I just sort of zone out on the cross on the pulpit.

After church ends, Grandma says that I can sit next to her and Grandpa and I can have a piece of gum if I sit still next Sunday. That's why we call her "Gum Grandma." I nod my head and fix my red and white polka dot dress. My white, scratchy tights are bunched up around my ankles because they are hand-me-downs from my much-older cousin. They have a hole in the toe, which is covered up by my scuffed dress shoes.

Just then, my dad says hello to Grandpa, who invites us to come over for lunch. Uncle Harold, Dad's brother, Auntie Rose's husband, is standing nearby, so Grandpa invites him to join us. Twenty minutes later, after Dad rounds all of us up, we are piled into the station wagon, again, and on the road.

It is fun visiting company after church, so I am excited. Maybe they will have ice cream! Or fun toys! When we get to our grandpa and grandma's house, we scramble out of the station wagon, and race off, all over their lawn. Their grass is luxurious because it is so well watered. In the desert, most grass is crunchy. But here, we can run free.

Uncle Harold stands at the window with his hands in his pockets. As the adults prepare the lunch table, a cassette tape with recorded church hymns plays in the background. "Tag, you're it!" I squeal at my brother, Sam. Then I run away from him as fast as I can, dress and blonde hair blowing in the wind and my soft feet kicking up behind me.

"Kids, it's time to come in for lunch!" Mom calls from the back patio door. We ignore her and keep running around the back yard. There is a pigeon pecking around in one of the flower planters. I love birds. Whenever I see one on the ground, I try to catch it. So I walk up to it slowly, so as not to startle it. I motion to my brother Sam to be quiet. He looks at me with wide brown eyes and sits down in the grass. I take another step. Then another. Stop. Wait.

The pigeon seems unconcerned with me, as it hops up onto the planter and struts along the top of it. I take a step and stop until I am close enough to reach out and touch the pigeon. But I pause for a few more moments and try to let the pigeon know that I am not going to hurt it. Very carefully, I extend my hands to the pigeon, and lay them on the planter in front of it, palms up. I smile at it, and it hops onto my hands. How excited I am! But I have to contain myself so it won't get startled and fly away.

I hold the pigeon and look at it. What a pretty bird—different shades of gray, with a shiny green neck. It is calm as it swivels its head. I kneel down beside Sam and put the pigeon on his lap. "It tickles!" He laughs, wiggling his legs. And with that the pigeon flies away.

As we have lunch together, our grandparents ask us kids how school is going. I linger to see if Claire or Sam will share something. But they don't. They are busily munching on the good food our grandparents have prepared: fried chicken, mashed potatoes, string beans, and warm biscuits.

My dad chimes in with a recent update on my behalf: "Bridget skipped first grade!" Everyone stops eating to hear details. Dad beams, and then pats me on the head. I look at everyone nervously and pick up my fork.

I try hard not to disappoint my mom and dad, or make them sad. I want them to always love me.

Chapter 9: Sticky Taffy

Day and night were practically indistinguishable as I rotated in and out of the hospital like through a revolving door, in between my caregiving split shifts. From start to finish, my days were about twice as long as the amount of time I could bill for. And there was no mileage reimbursement. I got people out of bed and ready for the day in the morning, I got them ready for bed at the end of the day, and everything in between. The girl in me, the mother in me, the woman in me, all swirled together like sticky taffy—different colors, different consistencies, and different flavors—all in one form, yet distinct.

Every two hours around the clock, no matter what else I was doing, I pumped my breast milk and stored it in small plastic containers that I labeled and froze until I could bring them to the hospital for later use. My breasts grew chapped and sore, and pumping became painful and wearisome. It hurt when they were full and I couldn't pump right away.

Some days, I sat in the rocking chair by Imani's Isolette and just breathed. Out the window, I could see glowing couples leaving with their babies. After being at the hospital for over a month, my initial adrenaline rush of combined terror and wonder had dissipated into a slow trickle of bewilderment and delirium.

At 8:00 a.m. on a late February morning, my alarm clock rang. With the rumble of a busy Minneapolis leaking in accompanied by sunlight through a cracked window, I slowly lifted my uncooperative eyelids to peer at my clock. But they couldn't manage to stay open.

"Aren't you going to work?" Jessica asked me, her voice sounding far away. "Bridge, it's ten o'clock!" Immediately, I sat up in bed, eyes bugged out and looking everywhere, still in my clothes from the day before.

"Holy shit! What happened?" I muttered. Untangling myself from my blanket, I sat up on the side of my bed and tried to orient myself. My breasts were engorged, and I had to pee.

With legs that felt more like tree trunks, I shuffled to the bathroom. Sitting on the toilet, I fantasized about sleeping. My first shift was at 10:00 a.m., so I didn't have time to take a shower. Luckily, it was only a bath visit up Franklin Avenue about ten minutes.

After pumping, I put nursing pads into my bra and put on a fresh shirt since I had leaked through the other one. My laundry basket was overflowing, and I was out of laundry soap and quarters. My refrigerator was empty, except for some expired milk. I slicked my dirty hair back into a ponytail with gel, grabbed my purse and keys, and headed downstairs. My stomach growled loudly, and I tried to ignore it as I huffed in a hurry, now that I was late for work and couldn't reach my client Matilda by phone to let her know.

Getting into my red Ford Taurus, I dumped my purse onto the passenger seat and turned the key in the ignition. It whined but wouldn't start, so I turned it a few more times—each time growing more and more frustrated and despairing. "Start, you mother fucking car! START!"

Pumping the gas pedal frantically, I continued to turn the key, causing the engine to screech incessantly—until a neighbor, Adam, stopped and said, "You're going to flood the engine if you keep giving it gas." He lived on my floor with his bleach-blonde-haired boyfriend and worked at a local theater.

"Let me get my jumper cables," he said. "I'll be right back.

I got out of my car and kicked the driver's side door. "You piece of shit!" Someone walking by on the street looked back at me as he kept walking, shaking his head. I wanted to punch him in the face.

While I waited for Adam, I had a moment to think about my day, which led to reflecting on what my life was now. Last summer, I was going to bed when I wanted to and waking up after a full night's rest. My only responsibility was work, and it didn't start until 10:00 a.m. or later. When I got home, I played with my cats and drank beer while I checked in with my friends to see what they were up to. I had regularly gone rollerblading around the Minneapolis lakes, explored, made love, and danced all night. It was curtain close on all of that.

Now I didn't even have time to pee or eat in peace, and I worried about the bills that came flooding in while I worked faster and harder but couldn't keep up. Life moved at lightning speed. There was no space to breathe or think or process anything. It was so much more than I had expected. I had envisioned myself going on with my life as I always had—that having a baby was like getting another sibling, and I had handled at least ten of those. How could it be so radically different from what I had imagined? Tomorrow was a complete unknown.

Adam returned with his jumper cables and asked me to pop my hood. I fumbled for the latch on the lower part of my dash on the left side of my steering wheel and gave it a yank with a sigh of relief. The day had hardly begun, and I was already physically exhausted and emotionally drained. Adam hooked up the jumper cables to his car and asked me to try starting it after a few minutes. After another false start, my car was running again. Adam had saved the day! This day. I didn't have time to reflect anymore; I had to get on the road to work.

Matilda didn't notice that I was late because she was watching one of her shows. I got her laundry going and made lunches for her for the next few days.

* * *

My second shift of the day was with a woman I had not met who needed a PCA to fill in for her regular person whose car had broken down. With an address and a few case notes I arrived at Mary's apartment on the seventh floor of a high rise in Minneapolis, where she lived with her daughter, Annie. Mary looked at me cautiously as she opened the door, wearing her nightgown and worn-out faded yellow slippers. "Hi," I said as I shifted my purse to my other shoulder so I could shake her hand.

I followed her into her apartment and put my purse down on a clear spot on her messy kitchen table. Mary walked into her bedroom and showed me where she kept her medications and medical supplies. "First, I need you to put on my cream," she instructed. Picking up the jar of heavy cream, I read the label that told me that it was for psoriasis. Mary wanted me to start applying the cream to her almost bald scalp, then her arms and legs. I did so with latex gloves, which I pulled off and threw away after I was done.

Annie came in from the kitchen, where she had been making a light lunch for her mother, and said that she needed her medication for her schizophrenia. Mary muttered something I didn't quite catch that seemed like an apology. "It's OK," I said, reassuringly. Mary shuffled toward the kitchen, her heels hanging off the backs of her slippers. Sitting down at the table, she put her napkin on her lap and thanked Annie.

After lunch, Mary asked me to change her bed and do her laundry. As I did, she made her way to her sofa, where she seemed to resign herself to something as she looked out the window at the Minneapolis skyline.

"It's a nice view," I mused, balancing a laundry basket on my hip.

"Yes, I love the city," she said, turning her head toward me slightly with a hint of melancholy. I wondered what she was thinking. *Did she struggle like Imani when she was a child? Would Imani's future mimic hers?*

* * *

When I got back to the hospital in the early afternoon, Karen was there, and she stretched out her arms to me. "How are you, honey?" she cooed, stroking my head. All I could do was rest my head on her chest like she was my surrogate mother or some version of a guardian angel or at least exactly what I needed.

"Ugh, it has been…" and I hugged her tighter.

"I was a single mom, too," she interrupted. "I will tell you about it sometime. My son is a great man now and in his forties, believe it or not. You are strong and you are a wonderful person. Really, you're going to be a great mom."

My eyes filled with tears, and I nodded, then left her embrace and walked over to the Isolette. I took a wet Q-tip and wiped Imani's mouth, since it got dry and chapped from the ventilator, and put it away in a small necklace box. In case she died, I wanted to have pieces of her.

On her white board, Imani's current weight was written: 3 pounds. Whispering through an open door of the Isolette, I told her, "I'm proud of you, Imani." She waved her hands as if she were acknowledging me.

Karen laughed and said, "That girl's a talker."

I tried to imagine what Imani was feeling, thinking, understanding, and enduring. I imagined her as a butterfly in an artificial chrysalis—yearning to break free of her tubes, wires, bright lights, and enclosed Isolette.

Does she know who she is? Who I am? How could she know that I'm her mother when there are so many other people hustling around her all the time? But she must know my voice from the twenty-six weeks that she was inside me. The times I read books to her, sang her songs, argued with Jessica and Marcus, talked to the people I worked with, bantered with people in the community as I did errands, and practiced Spanish.

Sitting down in the rocking chair beside her, I read aloud part of *Little Women,* so she would be exposed to literature. I hadn't finished it when I was young. Then I sang two songs to her: "Unchained Melody" because it was beautiful and soothing and I liked the part about coming home even though time goes by slowly and "Wild World" because it *was* a wild world, but we would make it.

* * *

Over two months into the NICU life, Imani's cares were starting to resemble those of a typical baby: she was moved to an open-air crib because she could regulate her own temperature and wore regular baby clothes. For a "micro preemie," she was doing exceptionally well, and I delighted in all her progress. Karen covered her with a blanket she had knit. She had also knit a larger one for when she went home. She told me that all the "kangaroo care" (skin-to-skin bonding) was paying off. Imani started to look more like a full-term newborn, too, as she had fewer wires attached to her and she was less scrawny. At long last, she had started drinking some of my stored breast milk from a small bottle.

I took notes on everything in my notebook to the point that I felt like an archivist: when she pooped, how much, what it looked like, how much she ate and at what time, what her vital signs were. I noted exactly what I would need to do to take care of her, what to watch out for, what different signals meant, how to handle the myriad of problems that would inevitably arise, like when she forgot to breathe…

Chapter 10: Pretty Pictures of Me

The sheets smell fresh on the clothesline, blowing in the wind. My sister and I have to hurry to take them down, as the air smells like rain, and the dark clouds are moving swiftly across the desert sky. I am almost seven years old, but tall. So if I stretch, I can reach the lower parts of the clothesline, where the laundry pulls it down.

"Claire, we should play hide-and-seek in here!" The sheets strewn along five lines make for a fluid maze—one that is whimsical and forgiving. Claire giggles at me and slips away through a flowery flat sheet. From within the billowing sheets that envelope me, I can't see her. Anyone outside the clothesline can spot us—our feet give us away. And the sound of our panting, which can't be helped, especially as it becomes more pronounced during our game. We chase each other around, big grins on our faces, which are hidden until we emerge, with raindrops pelting our heads, sliding from our hair. I lunge at Claire, tackling her to the ground, grass staining her pink shorts. She runs into the house yelling, "You can't catch me!"

When I get to my feet, I see that half-drooped over the chain link fence is a man who lives next door, and he takes his penis out of his shorts while staring at me. He puts it through the fence and waves me over. Stunned, I run into the house and tell my mom. She tells Claire and me to stay inside. We don't dare to look out the window to see when he goes away. Instead, we play in the house the rest of the day, with the curtains closed. Our dolls have a tea party as I try to forget the confusing sight I have seen on the perimeter of our sanctuary of childhood joy.

A few days later, I can't remember the incident and only know that my mom asks me to stay away from the fence.

* * *

The next Sunday after church, we visit Uncle Harold and Auntie Rose. They have an armored statue at the front door and fresh, lush grass just like Grandma and Grandpa's.

After lunch, I draw a picture of a flower on a Raggedy Ann and Andy Magic Slate Paper Saver—a cardboard drawing board, with a decorated border, and a plastic sheet that you could draw on with a stylus. When you lift the plastic sheet up, the drawing disappears.

"What are you drawing, Bridgie?" Harold asks me.

I don't answer.

"Let me make a picture for you. Watch," he says, taking the Magic Slate from me.

First, he draws the face of a woman, with long hair and big lips. Then he draws her arms and legs."

"Where is the rest of her body?" I ask Uncle Harold.

"Shhh, be quiet and you will see my whole picture when I'm done."

"OK, sorry," I apologize.

Next he draws a pregnant belly and asks me, "Does that look like your mommy?"

"Yes, my mommy has a baby in her belly."

"OK, now wait quietly while I draw the rest of your mommy."

He draws large breasts with big, plump nipples and adds pubic hair.

"This is a mommy," he explains. "She has a baby in her belly because she was in bed with a daddy."

"Harold, what are you talking to her about?" Rose asks meekly.

At that moment, Harold lifts the plastic sheet, erasing the picture he has drawn. "I'm showing her how to make drawings on this Magic Slate."

"Is that all he was doing, Bridgie?" Rose whispers to me, skeptically, leaning over the arm rest of her wheelchair. I nod my head as I look at Harold.

He laughs and puts the Magic Slate away. "We will have more fun with this another time, pretty girl."

The church doesn't let us be pretty, and it is a sin to try to be. But they still talk about who is pretty—and smart—and treat them special.

Chapter 11: Pomp and Circumstance

When the day came to go home, a nurse took a picture of me holding Imani with the hospital's Polaroid camera. She gave it to me, and I shook the square until the picture emerged. It was anticlimactic, but we were ready to go. Even though I had given birth to Imani, it didn't feel like my baby was mine. She seemed to belong to the hospital. *What in the world will I do without the staff?*

As I walked to the hospital parking lot once again, I was not empty-handed. It was a different exit than those I had watched out the fourth-floor window when other parents took their newborn babies home, with arms full of balloons and flowers. Today it was quiet. There was no fanfare. It was eerily like leaving work for the day and a few coworkers waving to you but most of the office continuing to work without looking up. But in my heart was a double rainbow.

In the parking lot I had parked in for three months without a baby in tow, I opened my car door, placing Imani in her car seat and buckling the seatbelt. When I first came to the hospital with Imani in my belly, it was a cold, dark winter day. Now it was a bright, sunny spring day. Birds were chirping, and people walked by wearing shorts and sunglasses.

Driving home on I-94, I clutched the steering wheel of my now properly functioning Ford Taurus and flinched at every movement around me—the big, loud trucks lumbering by, the fast sports cars driven by teenagers and men having midlife crises, and the clumsy, distracted drivers who were doing everything but looking at the road.

It was annoying as hell that people didn't get that I had a baby on board who was lucky to be alive and finally going home! I was tempted to flip them the bird, but that wouldn't be becoming of a mother. Clenching my teeth and breathing slowly, I stared at the Hennepin Avenue exit up ahead.

Fifteen minutes later, we were at my apartment building. Someone had parked in my assigned spot, so I had to park on the street and carry Imani and all of our things for two blocks up Dupont Avenue. I was sweating and cursing in my head, but I didn't want to let Imani hear me angry.

Once inside, I took Imani out of the car seat and held her close to my heart. I put my cheek next to her soft, pudgy cheek. Carefully, I turned her so she could see our studio apartment, with the king-sized converted waterbed with fuzzy blue covered bumpers in the middle of the room, the yellow paper suns strung along the perimeter of the ceiling, the radiator where we hung our jewelry and clothes, the dried up plant on the floor, the black vinyl sofa from a thrift store downtown, and the narrow kitchen with one counter and a twenty-year-old refrigerator at the end of it. Imani held my finger and looked alert, her blue eyes shining. Leaning my ear toward her, I double-checked that she was breathing normally.

As softly as I had spoken to Imani when she was first born, I said, "We are home now." I imagined showing Imani how beautiful life was.

Chapter 12: A Good Little Mother

Mom is pregnant again, and some of her friends are helping with packing for our move to Minnesota. There are already six children, and I am now eight years old. My brother Tommy is in a playpen because he is mischievous and climbs all over everything or runs off. Everyone helps my mom with the children, too, including me. There are always diapers to be changed and little ones to be fed and supervised and entertained. Instead of playing with my toys or reading, I am changing diapers and feeding the younger kids.

"Bridget, can you give Tommy some breakfast? He's getting whiny in his playpen."

"Bridget, will you check if David went to the bathroom?"

"Bridget, did Claire come back from the mailbox?"

"Bridget, what is Sam doing in the back yard?"

Sometimes I engage the children in games that I like, such as playing school or store. I teach them to read, and we pretend to have different jobs, like scientist, police officer, teacher, minister, or clerk.

"Kids! Let's play school," I command them. They love playing school because I give them "prizes"—toys we already have that I put into a pail and hand out for getting their answers right.

Claire, Sam, and Ryan sit on the bed in the bedroom that I share with Claire and wait for me to give instructions. David and Tommy are too young for playing school. Our bedroom is the best one because we have a bunk bed, stacked perpendicular, with a wardrobe in the space under the top bunk that is unoccupied by the bottom bunk. It is the perfect hiding place or spot when I need somewhere dark and quiet to go to shut out the world.

"Class, today we are going to do re-SEARCH (as I pronounce it when I am in scientist mode) on desert wildlife. I'm going to start with giving you a lesson on snakes in this region," I begin. "This lecture will be recorded so you may listen to it again to prepare for your exam tomorrow."

I rewind the tape in the black rectangular cassette player that lays flat on a small table, and press "record."

Claire, Sam, and Ryan sit patiently while I tell them everything I know about snakes in Arizona, which is a lot since I have been reading up on them in library books. They are good at sitting still and have long attention spans because we have to sit quietly in church for one to two hours at a time.

"Thanks for keeping the kids quiet, Bridget," Mom yells from the living room. "I have a lot of work to do and I don't feel very well."

"You can rest, Mommy. We're playing school right now, and they are doing their homework. They will have nap time after that."

"Good girl. You will make an excellent mother."

But I want to be a scientist…

Chapter 13: Homecoming

On a beige love seat, with pillows propping up my head, my feet hanging over the opposite armrest, still wearing a tight floral tank top and white shorts from the day before, I emerged from a dream to the realization that I had a baby on my chest. The apartment was quiet, except for the whir of the occasional car outside the window overlooking Hennepin Avenue. I thought about how traffic sounds like an orchestra, with the humming of the buses, the bass tempo of the big trucks, and the whirring of the cars going by at different pitches—with Minnesota road construction as the almost ever-present percussion.

Jessica was sleeping on her day bed in a pink, glittery tracksuit, clutching a stuffed animal. I woke up exactly as I had gone to sleep, with my hands still on my baby's back. She was in the same position, too. Scanning the air with her open mouth, she squirmed slightly, with a whimper. When my chest rose and fell with each breath, she rode the wave of my respirations as they reminded her to breathe, too.

It was very early in the morning, in late April, and it had been three months of constant upheaval and angst. But I felt ALIVE! Sleep deprivation from nights of pumping breast milk and visiting the hospital into the late hours after work seemed to dissipate as I held my treasured gift in my arms. I already had a sense of accomplishment as a mother. I had gone back to work shortly after my C-section, paid my bills, completed mountains of paperwork to mitigate financial crisis, and spent every day at the hospital in between shifts and into the night. If there was a motherhood boot camp, I had passed it like a champion. I could do anything going forward if I could get through all of that.

Then the phone rang, and it was Marcus.

"Hey."

"Hey, how's the baby?"

"She's good."

"Do you miss me?"

[shy laughter]

"Yeah, you know you do."

"I don't know."

"Of course you do."

"Mayyyyybe."

"Can I come over? You know you miss this dick."

"The baby is sleeping."

"Mmmmm I can fuck you with one hand over your mouth."

"I have to go."

"Why do you have to be like that? You're such a fucking bitch! Are you going to keep my baby away from me? You got someone over there? I'll break your fucking door down!"

"Nobody is here. I just need to rest."

"Well, you can rest on your back with my dick in you. Hahahaha!"

I checked on Imani in her crib and she was sound asleep; I'd be able to hide all the drama from her, for now.

* * *

Fifteen minutes later, Marcus opened the door to my apartment with the key I had given him when we were seeing each other (which he wouldn't return). Hearing the click in the lock, I stiffened and crossed my legs, clasping my hands on my knee.

Wasting no time, Marcus pushed me onto my bed and yanked my shorts off. "Give me that pussy," he snarled at me like he was a villain closing in on his prize.

Under his weight, I couldn't move, and he started to kiss me as he pulled my breasts out of my bra, then started to suck on my nipples. Getting one arm free, I tried to put my breasts back into my bra, but he pinned my arm down. "Stop fighting and enjoy it!"

Starting to panic, I looked at the crib, but Imani was still sleeping. "She's fine. Would you fucking stop being such a crazy bitch!" It seemed like he was right. Maybe I was overreacting; I did love him and wanted to be with him. He was my daughter's father, after all.

"Spray me with me your milk," he ordered. Looking toward the crib again, I tried to see if Imani was waking up.

That's when he grabbed my face. "You fucking dirty cunt, calm down and let me fuck you!" I didn't want to be difficult, and maybe I was getting uptight lately with all the stress I was under.

"OK, I'm sorry! I'll spray you with my milk and fuck you good."

"Finally! You were being such a damn prude, oh my God," he said, breathing heavily.

Getting into the character I thought he wanted me to be, I squeezed my breasts in his face, squirting him with milk. "Now you're being fun!" he snarled.

I also didn't fight when he dragged me to my shower and fucked me in the ass—even when I accidentally shit on him. Without washing his penis after having anal sex with me, he slammed me against the shower wall and put it in my vagina, but I didn't complain. I just wanted him to love me, so we could be a family. We had a beautiful baby together.

"I love you," I said.

"You're stupid." He laughed and dried off and put his clothes back on before walking out of my apartment.

Picking up my shorts and bra and throwing them into the laundry basket in the hallway to the bathroom, I walked to the shower. It hurt to wash my private areas, and there was still poop in the shower. As the hot water poured on my face, I wished it would either make me pure again or drown me. I loved Marcus, but he made me feel worthless. And there was something else eating at me. I was still unsettled about whether he was the father and horrified at the possibility of who else it might be.

Imani woke up, so I unfastened her sling that was attached to a crib wedge and picked her up. The wedge elevated her head, and the sling held her in place. She needed it since she still had gastroesophageal reflux disease (GERD), which caused discomfort and vomiting because her digestive system was still developing.

Jessica came home before I had to leave for work that afternoon. She sensed that something was off and asked me what was going on. I blamed it on being tired and asked if she could stick around until midnight when I got off work. Then she made me some chicken and pasta with Alfredo sauce, and I told her that we should forget guys and get married. She said she loved me like family and we could talk later if I wanted to.

The church taught that sex was sacred, and the purpose of it was to make babies.

Genesis 1:28: "And God blessed them, and God said unto them, be fruitful, and multiply and replenish the earth, and subdue it: and have dominion over the fish of the sea, and over the fowl of the air, and over every living thing that moveth upon the earth."

I had unwillingly done what the Bible said God wanted. Sex wasn't sacred, though. It was a pleasurable act when consensual, but it was also what men used to "have dominion" over women. Fuck what God wanted.

Chapter 14: On-Time Delivery

My aunt, Leah, who is only three years older than I am, lets me go with her on her paper route. "OK, Bridge, we're going to start going down County Road 721," and she speeds off on her ten-speed bike, throwing newspapers from her shoulder bag onto the driveways and front yards of rural homes in beautiful, forested northern Michigan. When we visit the ones who owe on their subscriptions, I can see in through the windows enough to sometimes get a glimpse of what their lives are like—lives outside of the church that I am intensely curious about. There are not so many kids running around, and they watch television and sometimes drink beer. They don't seem as bad as we have been told—not the wild and worldly people depicted in sermons and lessons. Even though we are told that we are God's special children, I feel that the unbelievers know more than we do about a lot of things because they aren't so sheltered. They get to talk to more people and go more places than we can. A lot of people think our church is weird, but I want them to accept me.

We sail through neighborhoods and down busy roads, occasionally seeing other kids on their bikes. They don't look like bad sinners; they look like regular kids like me. We sometimes say hello to each other, and I wish the church would let me play with them.

When we get back to my grandparents' house, we have freezies from the downstairs freezer while Grandma makes lunch. I wonder if unbelievers have grannies like mine who make them lunch—and why wouldn't they? Everyone has grannies. What do they do at home, and what do they talk about? If we never talk to them because they are unbelievers, then we are probably guessing what they are like. I want to talk to an unbeliever and learn about them. It doesn't scare me that they wear makeup and earrings and have smaller families.

Chapter 15: #3420

Opening my mail, I saw that I had more paperwork to do for Hennepin County to keep my food stamps and general public assistance. I still had some WIC (Women, Infants, and Children) vouchers to get some free milk and cheese.

It was early afternoon on a Friday, and I had exactly two hours to get to Human Services at Century Plaza (across from the Convention Center) in downtown Minneapolis before I had to get back to work. There was a parking spot at a meter, and I had seventy-five cents to feed it. I inhaled and hoped the line wasn't long.

Sure enough, the place was jumping. I pulled a number (3420) and waited. Looking around, I saw families and a lot of women—some with children.

Sitting a couple rows in front of me was a young woman, about my age, with an infant on her lap. She was stroking the baby's cheek. "Hi, sweetie, you're so beautiful."

"3411!" a man announced. The woman put her baby back in her car seat and gathered up her things. "3411!" the man announced again. "3412!"

Out of breath, she approached the man with her ticket and said, "I'm 3411."

"We're on 3412 now, so have a seat."

She sat back down with her bags and car seat while shuffling the paperwork she had brought in.

"3412! I'm calling 3412!" the man boomed.

Nobody came up, so he waved the young mother to a counter. Her baby started crying, and she put a pacifier in the baby's mouth, but the baby spit it out. I wondered how long they had been waiting for their turn. The baby cried louder, and I could see the mother trying to talk to the woman at the counter and gesturing to her paperwork. But she was turned away. As she walked past me to leave, I saw her already care-worn face as she shifted her car seat to her left arm, her baby wailing inside it.

Through the window, I could see her waiting at a bus stop where there were some men smoking cigarettes and passing a bottle around. One of them tried to talk to her, but she didn't engage. He must have gotten mad because I could see him yelling at her. She moved to the edge of the bus stop, but he followed her and pushed her. I wanted to help her, but I didn't have time to spare. Losing her balance, she almost dropped the car seat. The drunk man waved his arms at her, yelling something. The woman checked on her baby and went across the street, which was when I lost sight of her.

"3415!" the man called. A couple rounded up their kids and started for the counter.

"3415!" the man announced louder. The couple hurried up to the front, telling their small children to hurry. I could hear the woman at the counter ask if anyone had a job. The translator stated that the father had a job.

"What does he do for work?" the woman at the counter pressed.

"He's in construction," the translator replied.

"Well those guys make a lot of money. What are you doing here then?"

"He got injured and hasn't been able to work."

"Alright. Have them fill out this form, and we will process it in the next thirty days."

"3418!" An old woman shuffled to the service counter.

"3419!" "A middle-aged man went up.

"3420!"

I went to the counter and offered my paperwork, hoping that it would be satisfactory. The woman looked at me disapprovingly. "It doesn't look like you're working enough hours. See if you can pick it up because otherwise we will have to put you in our employment program. It's meant to help people become self-sufficient."

"But I'm working. I'm in home care, and I work a lot of split shifts."

"I'm not going to argue with you. You need to work on this, or your benefits will be in jeopardy. Keep saving all of your pay stubs so you can prove your income."

"Yes, ma'am."

Turning around, I saw the remaining people waiting: an old man with white hair in a braid, who looked like he lived on the street, talking to himself, a middle-aged woman with two children, a pregnant teenager who looked at the floor, a man in dirty clothes who looked like he had just come from a labor job, and a twenty-something mother with two small children. *Who are they?* I wanted to know them. If we had the opportunity to know each other, we could at least have some semblance of a community, like the church people who stuck together when they felt persecuted. Those of us in this office actually were persecuted—we were criminalized. I walked out of the building to check the parking meter. The traffic cop was two spaces down, and there was no ticket on my windshield.

I drove to meet Cole, and like every day, he descended the bus stairs and went past me without any acknowledgment toward his house. He had his snack and watched *The Simpsons*, and we did his physical therapy together. Today, he was bubbly, and every so often, he would half look at me and say, "Hi!" When I said "Hi!" back, he pushed out a laugh and flapped his hands. It seemed like a good day to visit the community center so he could play basketball. He ran most of the way there, and I had to keep up with him, which was easier now that my abdomen was healed from my C-section and not so tender.

After Cole's mom, Beate, came home and grumpily told me I was done, I went to see Matilda for a late bath visit. During bath time, she wanted me to sing with her while I washed her long gray hair, which she normally kept in a bun. She had raised a son as a single mother while working in a factory. When she talked, she waved her weathered, crooked hands, which I watched with admiration, sensing what they had accomplished. She had a happy spirit and loved to laugh with me.

We sang "Over the Rainbow" while I scrubbed her beautiful gray hair with lavender shampoo.

Matilda giggled. "My neighbors probably think there's a party going on over here." She told me that I looked like a movie star and insisted that I have some potato chips while she snacked from an open bag and watched *The Price is Right* on TV. Her apartment was cozy, and she seemed to feel right at home there, especially in her La-Z-Boy chair, parked in front of a large television with a wooden veneer and fuzzy reception. We lived in the same city, but our lives were so different—and yet, we were connected, like the string of paper suns that I had taped up around the ceiling in my apartment.

Chapter 16: Running Down a Dream

Lacing up my roller blades and yanking up my ribbed knee-high socks, I savor the smell of the fresh country air, then pop up from the cement slab in front of our green-painted house.

Swiveling my Body Glove fanny pack around my waist, so the pouch is in front, I stomp across the gravel driveway with my earphones around my neck. As I take off down the cul-de-sac, I switch my Sony Walkman to the tape setting. It has an auto-reverse feature, so I can listen to Tom Petty and the Heartbreakers' "Mary Jane's Last Dance" over and over again. Beyond the grasp of the church, out on the open road, I step one foot outside the fold.

Tom Petty's music is a new kind of spiritual, not the kind that makes me feel locked up and marked for Hell. It's like a church I want to go to, even though I don't understand its teachings—it's more about how it makes me feel. As the wind whips my hair and tightens my face, I think about what it would be like to be "Free Falling" and "Runnin' Down a Dream."

Clenching my thighs, and straightening my roller blades, I position myself for a straight descent down the middle of the paved road free of rocks or fear. I pass the house where the reserved track star gets on the bus—a small blonde high schooler I think is cute, but doesn't know I exist, who goes right past me straight to the back of the bus. Charlie is studious and athletic like me, but confident and popular like I am not. Every morning, I hope he will sit next to me. Crushing on him is my dark secret.

Then I zoom around the corner with the small house of the garbage man and his wife whose two boys I babysit. It's a place where I experiment with makeup and pose in front of their mirrored wall, asking myself if I am as beautiful as the soap stars I watch on their television.

"We won't be gone long," Carla had said the night before. "Dave just has to pick up a new lawn mower, and I'm going to have a few beers with some moms who also need a break before we lose it." She laughed.

Her life seems so much easier than the moms in the church since she has only two kids and can do whatever she wants.

Both boys are watching Full House *on television and don't seem to notice when the screen door slams shut. I open my purse and pull out pale eye shadow and lipstick that I had bought at Target, up the road from the church, when I said I was going to my cousin's house in between services.*

First I do one eye and compare how I look with and without eye shadow. Yes, I am much better with it on. Seductively, I apply my lipstick. One day, I will put on a full face of makeup and talk to a boy.

Chapter 17: No Place Like Home

Jessica's mom, Janice, agreed to let us move into her house in Coon Rapids with her for a total of $250 monthly rent. My full-time home care job was not enough to pay my $550 rent in the Minneapolis apartment, plus food, electric, phone, and especially childcare. It would have taken working about 80 – 100 hours per week, which was especially impossible with split shifts. And I didn't have the wherewithal to absorb Jessica's expenses when she quit another job or didn't get money from her family. Janice offered Jessica her old bedroom back and me the bedroom in the unfinished basement, where Jessica had once hidden evidence of her eating disorder. In a few car loads—we didn't own much, and I didn't even have a bed—we were moved in. Janice had a large black Lab puppy named Rocky that was strong enough to push us over if he caught us unaware. He also clawed up most of the house, and the walls in Janice's bedroom, where she sometimes kept him, were torn up through the sheetrock. We decided that Imani couldn't be out of the bedroom, except to go in and out of the house. One pounce could kill her. One day, after we had been living there for a few weeks, I asked Janice if she could keep the dog outside, but she refused.

"It's my house, and I'm not keeping my pet outside," she insisted.

"The only reason I'm asking is because Imani isn't safe when he's in here. Maybe he could be out when we want to leave the bedrooms," I proposed.

"I'm not having a teen welfare mom talk to me like that, so if you don't like it, you can leave."

"Not sure how you can think I'm a welfare mom when I work. Kind of unbelievable that you can say that when you have been stealing my food. Your ass is getting fat on my food stamps."

"Well, considering the state paid for it, it wasn't yours anyway. Go get pregnant again and get more welfare, you slut."

"You just sit in your bedroom eating a teen mom's government aid."

"If you don't shut up, I'm calling the cops, and then you can go to jail while your baby rots in my basement."

Sitting down at the piano, I started playing as loudly as I could while she screamed louder and louder at me. My blood was boiling, and it was all I could do to distract myself and piss her off even more for messing with me. Then she snatched her cordless phone and went outside while I kept on playing. A few minutes later, the police showed up and I saw her mouthing her grievances and gesticulating toward the bay window on the second floor where I was watching the two police officers listening and taking notes.

Janice came back into the house with the two police officers, and they went upstairs to where I was sitting at the piano.

"Have you been drinking?" the twenty-something male cop asked me.

"Nope, I'm just playing the piano," I snarked.

"I hear that you have been disrupting this household and you just moved in here. This nice woman doesn't want any problems," the older balding male cop stated.

"Yep."

"We didn't see a criminal record, and you don't want one."

"All I did was ask if she can keep the dog away from my baby!" I told them as I suddenly started crying.

"I understand that you're emotional right now," the older officer said stoically, "but you need to obey the rules of this house and do what this homeowner says."

"You don't even know what happened and you're just listening to her because she's the homeowner and has more power!"

The younger cop interjected, "I think you may have some issues and you're overreacting. I would recommend looking for another place to live. There are plenty of apartments."

"Exactly," the older cop agreed. "You have a choice here."

That wasn't exactly true. I had tried to get onto a Section 8 waiting list, so I could move into my own place with Imani, but the wait was impossibly long, and it wasn't guaranteed that I would get anything. Nothing else was affordable for a caregiver who was a single teen mom with a disabled baby and a roommate for a babysitter. There wasn't much housing for complex lives.

Imani was crying from the playpen in the basement bedroom, so I abruptly left to take care of her. As I went down the stairs, Janice thanked the officers. "I really appreciate your help. These young single moms are kind of crazy."

"No problem, ma'am," the older cop said. "We see it all the time. No father around and cycling through the system. They need to make better decisions. Hope you can have a relaxing evening now."

Locking my door behind me, I picked up my six-month-old baby, who was less than ten pounds, and hugged her. "Nobody understands but us, sweetheart." Sometimes I told people that I had cloned myself as a smartass reply to the inquiries about who and where the father was and what he was doing.

Chapter 18: Forbidden Fruit

"Leave me alone!" I yell at my parents. I am fifteen years old.

"Change your outfit," Mom scolds me. "You look like an unbeliever." I am wearing a tight, pink, cropped tank top and cut-off, ripped jean shorts. My lipstick hue is a little brighter than the packaging had indicated.

"You wish you could pull this off; stop being jealous and let me live my life," I snap back. She is stalling me on my way to meet up with a couple of girls from church who are on their way to pick me up. My parents know their wild reputation.

"Maybe you need another lecture because yesterday didn't seem to sink in," Mom threatens. "And if you have money for lipstick, you can start paying for your own groceries."

Whipping around, I light a cigarette. Blowing a defiant puff of smoke into the air and rolling my eyes, I go out the front door, wishing I never had to go back.

As I walk outside, I hear my mom say to my dad, "She's a bad example for the other kids; we can't have her here anymore. And she's making us look bad at church."

"Keep talking about me!" I yell at Mom. "You think I'm going to just do what the church says like I have no brain, and it doesn't make any sense! It's my life, and the church can't control me!"

"She's so rebellious and nasty," says Mom.

"Yeah," says Dad.

"If she wants to live here, she has to follow the rules," she continues.

"You're right," Dad agrees.

"OK, I raised all your kids that the church told you to have, and now you just kick me out because you got what you wanted and you have other babysitters!" I say in my defense.

"People used to tell us that we were lucky to have such a helper, but not anymore. Nobody actually does much to help around here, and you should be happy to help your family," Mom criticizes.

"Whatever, bitch," I curse, as I go back outside and light another cigarette in disgust.

When I come back inside, I go directly downstairs to my bedroom and touch up my makeup. Fuck them, I think. Kissing my oval mirror and throwing double middle fingers, I pose like I'm Joan Jett.

* * *

In between church services, we are celebrating Christmas in the church basement with our family on my dad's side. I am wearing a modest, baggy sweater with a red and green pattern. I am not feeling well; I feel empty and unwanted. It is like I am under water—everyone is talking and laughing, and I can't understand them. Christmas had always excited me, but not this year. My aunts, uncles, and cousins are mingling and noshing near the kitchen area, where there is a wide L-shaped counter where food is served. Exhausted, I flop into a chair near the bookstore, by the stairs, and think about dying. Life is a dark tunnel leading nowhere, and nobody cares. If only I could go to sleep and not wake up and just walk out the back door, leaving the party and everything else for good. It is doubtful that anyone would miss me.

On the way home, I ride in the back of my parents' long, white van, which rattles and shakes as it lumbers down the road full of children—arms hanging out of windows, bodies sprawled out on the floor in the back, and the inevitable squabbles. Over each bump in the road, with worn out shocks, I bounce and slouch further down on my bench seat. But I am still here. A couple of the younger kids are fighting over a new toy and battle across my lap until I grab it and throw it into the back. They chase it like dogs playing fetch. What is all the hype about being a teenager? Parents at church tell us to enjoy our youth, but they put us to work. They tell us to appreciate it because being an adult is harder. But instead it feels hollow and gray and icky. Will my whole life feel like this?

Recently, my boyfriend and I had broken up. He was almost thirty years old and told me that he had been a model in Italy when he left the church for a few years. I met him in the parking lot of the church where all the teens and singles hung out and smoked. He had invited me to his house, where I had sex for the first time when I was seventeen. I wanted to see what it felt like because I didn't know anything about intercourse. Church girls talked about it to each other, and we all wondered what happened. What we did was a sin because we weren't married. But we kept having sex anyway, and I lied to my parents about where I was.

Pulling into the driveway, all the younger kids rush toward the sliding van door, vying for the first chance to jump out. Dad looks at me in the rear-view mirror and says, "Shape up your attitude. It's Christmas." I say nothing and climb out the front passenger door because the sliding door is clogged with kids who are in my way. Dad comes into the house and lights a cigarette by the kitchen range hood fan and hovers over the stove as he smokes. He doesn't notice as I take a bottle of acetaminophen out of the cupboard and pour myself a glass of water. Exasperated, I take a handful of the pills and swallow them. Dad glances slightly in my direction but doesn't care what I am doing. Mom walks in and lights a cigarette out the kitchen window without looking at me.

"I swallowed the rest of these pills," I say as I thrust an empty pill bottle at my parents, waiting for them to shut down my body and release me from my miserable life.

"What did you do that for?" Dad admonishes. My mom immediately calls 911.

Dad drives me to the emergency room, my mom sitting and crying with me in the back seat of the car. After a few hours I am discharged with information on therapists for depression and anxiety. I start taking anti-depressant medication to help with my low energy and mood regulation and "acting up." Mom drives me to my appointments and asks a lot of questions. During one of our conversations, she tells me that she has started seeing a psychologist. "I'm depressed, too," she confides in me.

Chapter 19: Lawyers and Money

Marcus filed papers in a Minneapolis court for custody. I was panicked. He had told me numerous times that he would take my baby away from me, even though he didn't show any effort to actually take care of her.

It took some doing to rearrange my work schedule, but I was able to coordinate a time to meet with my lawyer, Matt Cunningham, at his office. My parents agreed to lend me money to pay him, and I could also work some of it off by babysitting. My dad was a welder, and my mom was a nurse now, and both of my parents made a decent living. He asked me about my history with Marcus, going back to the very beginning.

"We hooked up a few times, and I got pregnant. Then he started raping me," I said. "He let himself into my apartment in Uptown with keys I had given him, sometimes in the middle of the night. It happened a lot. He would come through the door, push me down and start undressing me."

Over the next couple of hours, I told Matt everything, and he filed a motion that described our "relationship marred by violence."

On July 12, 1999, Marcus and I appeared in court together—he as the plaintiff (pro se) and I as the defendant with my lawyer, Matt. The drive was over an hour from Foley in my gas-guzzling, big, long, brown 1978 Lincoln, which I had bought from an old man in a trailer park on a handshake payment plan for $800.

Foley was a small, rural town near St. Cloud where I was able to find subsidized housing and moved with Jessica and her sister Valerie. Valerie joined Jessica in babysitting Imani, and I paid for living expenses for all three of us. We also fought like this: Valerie vs. Jessica, Bridget vs. Jessica, Valerie vs. Bridget, Bridget vs. Jessica and Valerie. We all loved Imani, but we were like oil and water in our subsidized two-bedroom apartment, which cost $310 per month. The strain of holding the entire household together was oppressive. I rarely slept and, in addition to working, I also had to take on the roles of fixer for any household problem and mother to three. Valerie had chronic sinus infections and no health insurance, so I faked having them and got medication for her. She also liked to go out a lot when she wasn't babysitting and needed spending money that I had promised I would give her. Jessica constantly needed rides to one place or another and had regular meltdowns when she didn't have her way. When we were low on groceries, it was on me to go to the store. Every time my car broke down, I was the one responsible for fixing it, since it was mine and I had the job to go to.

Marcus looked very serious and fidgety, and I thought it must have been the first time I had ever seen him acting nervous, like he was outnumbered. The judge addressed him first and clarified the purpose of the hearing: we were there about custody. Marcus, fumbling, leaned toward the microphone and said, "Yes, Your Honor, yes." He then clasped his hands tightly and stared at the table.

"Your Honor," Matt began. "My client is seeking sole physical and legal custody, per the domestic abuse allegations detailed in my motion. She is afraid and doesn't feel that her daughter is safe with the plaintiff."

Marcus interrupted, standing up, "Your Honor," he stammered, grasping for the decorum of the situation, "Bridget is a liar. I never did what she said. Imani is my daughter, and I have the right to see her. Bridget is playing games to keep her away from me."

"Mr. Vega," the judge stopped him. "You will have your turn to speak. Mr. Cunningham has the floor. It is the defendant's chance to speak. Wait a few minutes, please."

"Ms. Siljander, is it correct that you earn $1,030 per month working for Express Personnel Services in Saint Cloud?" the judge asked.

"Yes, that's right, Your Honor. I do temp work full-time," I replied. For the past several months, I had been working temp jobs because one of the people I was a PCA for was abusive and there were no other openings at the home care agency that would give me enough hours.

"And, Mr. Vega, is it correct that you earn $1,106 per month as a bouncer at Bunkers Bar & Grill in Minneapolis plus some self-employment?" The judge turned to Marcus.

"Yes, Your Honor," Marcus responded.

"Mr. Vega, do you admit in open court that you are the father of the child in this case?" the judge asked.

"Yes! I know I'm the father. She looks like me, and when my family seen her, they said the same thing."

"OK, then I will document this in the court filing," he said.

"Your Honor, can I still get a paternity test?" Marcus continued. "Bridget lies, and I want to make sure." He squinted his eyes at me angrily.

"Of course," the judge assured him. I was aghast that Marcus would request a paternity test when he had been so adamant that Imani was his child and that nothing could stop him from being her father. Yet, I was relieved that the ball was in his court and that I didn't have to request the test. Soon I would find out the truth.

* * *

At our next hearing, we reviewed the paternity results that had come in the mail.

"Mr. Vega, the blood tests show a likelihood of paternity of 99.817 percent. Are you satisfied with this result?"

Although I had been quite sure that this would be the result, I still let out a sigh of relief. How could I have ever told my family if Imani's father was the other possibility? What would this have meant for Imani?

Marcus shifted anxiously, his eyes darting about. "So that means I am definitely the father?" he asked.

"Yes," the judge replied. "You are definitely the father. We don't get results that say 100 percent. This is as high as it gets. That is your daughter."

Marcus groaned in frustration. "Then I want to go forward with everything so I can see my daughter. I am going to be in her life!"

I looked at Matt, who showed no nonverbal body language I could read to indicate his reaction. It had to be good, I thought. It looked like Marcus was coming to terms with his being a father. We had been young, after all. He was only twenty-two when I got pregnant.

Glancing at Marcus again, I could see that he had tears in his eyes. We were across the courtroom from each other in a contentious battle. However, we were there for Imani, I thought to myself. It seemed possible that we could even be a family. I still loved him. With every fiber of my being, I wanted it to work.

The Court ordered Marcus to pay $232 in monthly child support to address Imani's financial needs, including special health and educational expenses, keeping in mind a standard of living appropriate to the circumstances of both parents. This basically meant that the court considered the income of both parents in calculating child support and our mutual right to an adequate standard of living.

He would also need to reimburse the government for public assistance that I had received to help me care for Imani, in the amount of $1,365. Additionally, he would need to pay arrears at a rate of $46 per month—back to when Imani was born.

Marcus' health care contribution was ordered in the amount of $50 per month, and his day care contribution was to be $97 per month. Considering each expense alone could cost several hundred per month, it was a paltry contribution. It was his responsibility to file a motion if he wanted it to be reduced or suspended, which he was within his rights to do.

If Marcus had contributed his portion financially, I would not have needed public assistance, except medical. And he had been the one pushing me not to have an abortion.

I had sole physical custody, and we shared legal custody, subject to Marcus' right to supervised visitation. If he complied with supervised visitation, we would transition to family supervised visitation and eventually independent—with the court order stipulating who would be doing the pickups and drop-offs.

It was a giant relief to have our parameters defined and loosely resolved. Supervised visitation meant I could protect Imani from Marcus, even temporarily; it afforded me time. And I hoped that he would pay child support so I could have more of a normal life with her. There was a duality to my feelings for him—the love and longing, the grief and fear. I saw his humanity: the hurt little boy whose father abandoned him, the charming social butterfly who everyone was drawn to, the new father who flashed his love at his little girl, the brief moments of self-awareness and motivation to be a better person. I waited for these moments. It was like waiting for him to ask for his sins forgiven in the church. I didn't want to be one of the people who gave up on him during his worst of times, like people had with me. And, I wanted Imani to have a daddy who loved her as much as my daddy did when I was little, before there were so many children.

* * *

On the day of the first scheduled visit, I parked my old brown Lincoln on my designated side of Genesis II, the supervised visitation facility, opposite the side that Marcus parked on a half hour earlier. We were not allowed to see each other during supervised visitation.

Crawling into the spacious, velvety back seat, I unbuckled Imani and pulled her out. She was warm and smiley in her pink fleece coveralls.

"Uh! Uh!" She motioned as she twisted herself back toward her car seat and Worm Guy, her stuffed inchworm. Holding her on my right hip, I leaned in to fetch him for her. She giggled and shook him so he rattled and gave him a kiss.

"Are you going to see Daddy?" I asked her, pushing my forehead against hers. She was preoccupied with Worm Guy.

Inside, I handed off Imani to a supervisor who would observe her and Marcus for the next two hours. Even though the supervisors were trained and there were safety procedures here, it was still tough to separate from my little girl and not be able to see where she was or what was happening.

This was not the life I had imagined for my beautiful daughter, but I would fight for her. My car was a big junker, but I would upgrade it, and move out into my own apartment, and go back to college, and keep going as far as I could. I would get past all this and follow through on my promise to give her everything.

Under my breath, I said stubbornly to myself, "Fuck you, poverty; fuck you, adversity; fuck you, pain."

I was a force to be reckoned with if I could remember that I was already a survivor. Nothing could stop me unless I let it, and I sure as hell had to keep moving. Maybe one day I would still become a scientist. And if Imani wanted to be one, too, I would help her no matter what.

Chapter 20: Bottom of My Class

After biology lab at college, my lab partner, Troy, invites me to hang out with him at Champps, a restaurant by the Ridgedale Mall, which I go to often with my church friends. I have been crushing on him all semester. It is my second year of college, and I am seventeen years old. I think he told me that he's twenty-seven. It's flattering that an older, good-looking college student is showing an interest in me and treats me like I'm older. Instead of being a stupid church freak, I feel like a beautiful woman.

After a bit of small talk, he offers me a drink. I tell him that I've never had a drink in a bar before, or anything besides beer.

"Here," he says. "It's a White Russian—hardly any alcohol, and it tastes like ice cream."

I take a sip, and it's creamy and sweet, and it actually does taste sort of like ice cream. Troy smiles at me as I finish my drink, and I am proud to be sophisticated.

"See, they go down real smooth," he encourages me. "Let's get you another one."

Three or four drinks later—I have lost count—I feel the booze hit my brain like a tidal wave, and I also have to pee. Troy waits at the table while I try to walk straight and act like I'm fine. I'm dizzy, and everything looks strange, and I don't know what to do, hoping I don't embarrass myself. Looking at a blurry reflection of myself in the bathroom mirror to touch up my lipstick, I sway and try to hold my hand steady. Some lipstick gets on my face, and I swipe at it to get it off.

"There you are, babe," Troy says to me when I get back, not acknowledging how drunk I am. He pulls a chair out for me, and I

hold onto the table as I flop down. Troy is talking to me, but I can't follow what he's saying and look perplexed at his mouth moving to seem like I'm keeping up with the conversation. Then he stands, comes over to me, and helps me up. We make our way out of the bar.

He says goodbye to the bartender, and I see that we are the only people in the place now. A sports anchor is commenting on the latest Vikings game on the television above the bar, and the bartender is wiping glasses. I try to stay up on my feet and not let him notice my condition because I feel cheap and inexperienced.

Troy opens my car door for me, and I drag my body into the front seat. He sits in the passenger seat and makes conversation, but I don't say anything. My stomach starts churning, and a sickness pulsates in my whole body, and I groan. Troy grabs under my back to sit me up, and pushes my head out my window. I puke down the side of my car and onto the parking lot.

"Let it out," he says. "Now you'll sober up." When he lets go of me, I collapse sluggishly onto my seat, unable to move.

A few minutes after I puke, I stop groaning. Troy's hands move around inside my shirt and reach under my bra. He lifts my shirt up and sucks my nipples. I'm still quiet and motionless. He slides me down in the seat and spreads my legs open. For an amount of time that I can't estimate, he fucks me hard with his fingers. Then he turns my head to the side and climbs out of my car and drives away.

Sometime in the night, I wake up half-delirious with a wicked headache and drive home. As quietly as I can, I turn on the hose in the front yard and clean the driver's side door of my car. Feeling guilty and jittery about what has just happened, I open my bedroom window to let in fresh air and try to sleep before my high school graduation that afternoon. When I wake up, very hung over, I try to get the puke smell off with a long shower and mouthwash and perfume. The shame sticks to my insides, and I put on a smile for the occasion and the many photos. And I tell nobody.

Chapter 21: Gotta Live Too

When I parked in Cubby's guest spot in his townhome neighborhood and put the car in park, the shifter fell into my lap. Not wanting to delay my new assignment and being dedicated to utmost professionalism, I put the shifter on the floor and walked confidently to Cubby's front door, ready to work.

Gigi, his seventy-nine-year-old mother, opened it before I could ring the doorbell, dressed in a red, flowing dress, which looked fabulous with her white bobbed hair and red lipstick. "You must be Bridget." She greeted me warmly, with an air of elegance, ushering me toward Cubby, who was lying in his hospital bed in the living room.

"Hi, Cubby," I said. "What would you like me to do first?" Cubby had silver hair, which was parted on the right side and brushed in a wave toward the left. He was tan and wore tortoise shell glasses and a Polo golf shirt. It was enchanting and relaxing to be in their posh townhome with its cream carpeting, city-scape paintings on the walls, and French furniture. Especially with all the chaos in my life. Since falling out with Valerie after Jessica moved out, I had moved back in with my parents and was commuting an hour to work nights in a factory and was keeping up my daytime temp jobs. Imani had been sick a lot, and we were constantly rushing to the doctor. There was no room in my schedule for sleep, and I had gotten in a bit of trouble for writing bad checks to finance a medical billing company I tried to start with desperate hopes of working from home to be more present as a mom. I told

Cubby and Gigi that their back yard on the neighborhood pond looked like the French Riviera, and they were tickled. Cubby said that he sat out there a lot because the sun was good for his multiple sclerosis. That explained the tan.

"I don't want friends," Cubby said. "I need a caregiver who will do a good job and work hard to please me."

"Absolutely," I reassured him. "I'll make sure you're taken care of."

"All right then, I need you to listen to me closely because I'm going to tell you exactly what I need you to do." He reminded me of Mark.

"You got it."

"I do a pivot transfer. Do you know what that is?"

"Yes, I learned about it in nursing school. Do you want me to get you to a standing position and then pivot you to your wheelchair?"

"Very good. And make sure you brace my knees. I'll talk you through it."

"Do you want to get up now?"

"On the next commercial break, you can get me in the chair. Then I want you to take me to the laundry room and put me on the commode chair."

"Sounds good, Cubby."

Much of caregiving is what nurses, and sometimes even doctors, once did but handed off somewhere over the past fifty years: physical therapy exercises, managing medication, eating, transferring, positioning, bathing and dressing, toileting, and observing health status. It still was not regarded as a profession, even though it entails medical, intimate, and complex care and support that can be physically and emotionally challenging to perform.

Cubby and I watched *Meet the Press* together while I waited for him to instruct me to transfer him. He didn't talk during his television shows and didn't want anyone else to talk either. We all sensed this and tried to be quiet.

"Fuck these Republicans," Cubby said, breaking the silence. "They're all a bunch of assholes."

"Yes, they are," Gigi reiterated from the kitchen as she dried dishes from breakfast, holding her arms in a big circle above her head—"Giant assholes."

"She's not really a Democrat," Cubby muttered.

"My family is all Republican," I disclosed, without knowing what it meant. Growing up in the church, I was not exposed to politics, except to be told that we were not to vote for anyone who supported abortion.

Cubby shot me an inquisitive look. "Well, you don't look like a Republican to me, and that's a good thing."

That's when *Meet the Press* went to commercial break and I got back into work mode. Cubby showed me how to raise the head of his hospital bed with a handheld control. Then I swung his legs over the side of the bed, so he was sitting, facing toward me.

"On the count of three, I want you to stand me up," Cubby said.

I nodded.

"One, two, three."

I grabbed him in a hug and pulled him up off the bed. Our faces were close enough to each other that I could feel his breath. Remembering what I had learned in nursing school, I turned him forty-five degrees, so he was in position to sit in his wheelchair.

"OK, sit," Cubby prompted. And slowly, I lowered him into his wheelchair, which was locked. Carefully, I swung the leg rests into position as I lifted each leg. Cubby smiled at me, his messy gray hair sticking out like he was Einstein. He had charismatic energy and sparkling blue eyes that searched my face with curiosity.

"You're really smart, I can tell already," Cubby stated. "What are you doing in your situation? I want you to tell me the story."

Feeling subservient and not wanting to jeopardize my good first impression, I explained politely, "It didn't work out with my daughter's father, but he loves her. She's the best baby and she has such a cute personality."

"Does he ever see her?"

"Once in a while, he does, but we're not together anymore."

"Does he pay child support?"

"Not really, but he doesn't have a stable job."

"What does he do?"

"He works in restaurants, and I think he's a bouncer downtown."

"Well, those people make enough money to pay child support. He sounds like a dirt bag."

"Last time I talked to him, he said, 'I gotta live, too.'"

"What a loser; I'm going to call him 'Gotta Live Too.'"

Not disagreeing with Cubby, and surprised and thankful for his immediate support of me, I nodded. Mark would've liked him. We talked throughout the day and made a deal: I would work all of his shifts, and he would pay me enough to move into my own apartment; his schedule would meet his needs and give me time to go back to college. I was elated. I had promised Imani that I would get my degree and build a safe and happy life for us. More than that, though, the little girl who wanted to be a scientist was still in the running.

Chapter 22: Exhaling Faith

"In the name of the Father and the Son and the Holy Ghost. Amen." These are sweet words—because they mark the end of the sermon. A bunch of kids from Minneapolis and other church locations are in Detroit for the wedding of a couple we know from national church services. We are staying with church families, and I am looking forward to visiting Auntie Rose again. Her rheumatoid arthritis has progressed, and she has been living in a group home in a nearby suburb to be closer to her sister after Uncle Harold divorced her.

In the last year, before I graduated from high school, I had quit the church, but I was back with reluctance because leaving had been too disconcerting. As soon as I had said I was "giving up my faith," everyone suddenly treated me differently, like I was an alien from outer space. Many found my address in the church phonebook and sent me letters warning me of the risk of eternal damnation and urging me to repent while I still had time. Even my friends acted like I was a stranger as they tiptoed around me and asked why I wanted to leave. Confused and suddenly having a sense of being estranged from the only society I had ever known, I defaulted back to the church and its comforting social network.

As I leave the sanctuary, to extricate myself from church rituals, a young mom holding a baby, with a small child latched onto her leg, turns to me timidly and robotically says, "I'm glad you've returned to the flock of Jesus, Bridget. This is where you belong." Her face is washed out, and there is a sorrow in her demeanor. With a brief pause in my stride, I nod awkwardly and look down. I don't want to be here, but I don't know how to leave yet.

* * *

The day of the wedding, I park in front of Auntie Rose's group home and knock on the door. It is a small house with a few flowerpots in front and a newspaper on the step.

Inside, there is a living room, dining room, and kitchen. Down the hallway are three bedrooms.

An aide—a tall, slim man named John with sandy brown hair and a thin moustache—takes a break from making dinner for the housemates and leads me to her. She is lying on her bed and another aide—a pretty woman named Sheila with bright pink lipstick—is gently stretching her legs.

"Hi, Auntie Rose," I greet her quietly, so as not to surprise her. "Long time, no see."

Sheila lowers her leg and Auntie Rose turns to look at me with her kind eyes and a pleased and joyous expression that conveys how much she has missed me. It has been nine years.

"Oh my, you have grown, little Bridgie," Auntie Rose declares in her soft voice. "You are so beautiful!"

"You're the beautiful one, Auntie Rose," I echo affectionately. She is thin and frail with short, thin, curly hair. I am struck by how fragile she looks and how she seems to have shrunk, how her eyes look at me with the same familiar tenderness that makes me feel seen. When she speaks, she raises her shoulders as though she is trying to expand her bony chest to take in more air.

While we reminisce and I update her on my family, Sheila puts on her compression stockings and shoes as she lies in bed.

"I still have the kitty sweatshirt you made me in high school that says 'I Love You, Bridget,'" I remind her.

She fixes her sweet expression on me and barely above a whisper says, "Do you have the macramé owl I made you?"

"I wear it all the time," I say. "And I keep it in my jewelry box on the top tier."

Uncle Harold had laughed at her and said that it was a waste of time because she was "crippled." Once he left her home alone when he went on a business trip, and she wasn't able to take care of herself. A single woman from church came to visit her and discovered that she had been in bed for two days and living off of saltine crackers and water she drank from a pitcher with a long straw. That woman stayed with her until Uncle Harold came back, and he was furious that she had intruded.

"How about we go to the Ann Arbor Hands-On Museum?" she asks. "I want to show it to you."

"That would be really fun," I say as I watch Sheila lift Auntie Rose from her bed to her wheelchair and straighten her clothes. Her wheelchair has a custom seat cushion, and Sheila adjusts her to fit in it perfectly.

"She's ready for the wedding!" Sheila announces as she takes the brakes off of Auntie Rose's chair.

I cross my hands on my chest with a gesture of gratitude and thank Sheila for how well she takes care of my Auntie Rose.

"You are so welcome." She smiles. "She's a great lady." Then she looks at Auntie Rose fondly.

A few minutes later, a paratransit bus pulls up in the driveway of the group home and the driver gets out and comes to the front door. She is a middle-aged woman dressed in a company uniform and wearing a hat with a ponytail out the back.

Sheila pushes Auntie Rose to the front door and opens it. "You are always right on time, Mary Jo! I think you should train the rest of 'em to get their act together," she says humorously but seriously.

Mary Jo chuckles as she backs Auntie Rose out the front door and down the short ramp on the side of the step. "I'm just the little guy, ya know!" she says. "You get 'em to listen to me, and I'll set 'em straight!"

The two women laugh with a shared recognition of their place in society as people in low-status jobs. I am used to the church people talking about being marginalized by society—not "unbelievers." Could it be that other people feel like they are treated as inferior? I had thought that "unbelievers" could live how they wanted because they didn't have the confines of the church.

Mary Jo ties down Auntie Rose's wheelchair in the bus using straps and buckles that fasten to the floor. "This is so her wheelchair don't move around during transport," she explains. I sit on a seat across from Auntie Rose. We are the only people on the spacious bus.

Through the Ann Arbor neighborhoods we go. It could have been a suburb of Minneapolis. Auntie Rose grimaces as we bounce along but appears to be intent on riding out the terrain. So I don't say anything and absorb the sights as we pass them. Mary Jo's radio sounds periodically with an unintelligible mixture of static and voices.

Dressed up wedding guests are descending on the church when we arrive, and I feel a flash of anxiety about going in and seeing new people—especially the being on display part. Nobody wants to be caught in the "Pick-A-Little, Talk-A-Little" at church, and I know everyone thinks I am strange and wild. Mary Jo lowers Auntie Rose on a lift that extends from the side of the bus and lets me take the handles of the wheelchair. I straighten my fitted black dress and start for the entrance. Singing has already begun and is wafting out of the sanctuary.

A couple of people move further down their bench so I can sit down and park Auntie Rose next to me out of the way of traffic. We say, "God's Peace," like we always do when we meet other "believers." Auntie Rose asks me to forgive her sins.

"Believe all your sins forgiven in Jesus' name and precious blood," I say, putting my young hand on her emaciated shoulder. She nods, and I feel a spiritual connection between us.

"I wish I had the song book cover you made for me so we could sing together from your gift," I whisper in her ear. I look at her hands, which have made all those things and written all the elegant letters for me. They are clenched into fists now, and her crooked fingers have not written letters in several years. But to me, they are the most beautiful hands I have ever seen.

Chapter 23: Learning to Fly

Holding onto a child-sized walker, Imani scampered along the sidewalk with her chubby little legs in Hello Kitty leg braces and light-up sandals. She was wearing one of her favorite outfits: red shorts and a ruffle blouse with tiny red and pink flowers on it.

Her first physical therapist said that she would never walk without assistance because her hips were too tight—that she would always need a walker or something for stability. But I didn't worry about it. I knew that Imani would reach her own potential in her own time, and whatever it would be would be good enough. I knew my baby better than anyone else, and nobody could tell us what she couldn't do. And I was prepared to fight for her to give her the best life possible.

Imani had "graduated" from the NICU Follow Up Clinic, was discharged from her eye specialist, and was on track developmentally, according to what was considered "normal." The NICU Follow-Up Clinic monitored across several areas of growth, such as intellectual and developmental milestones. Her IQ tests and other assessments indicated she was on track.

She was doing amazingly well for a micro preemie and high-risk infant. There were no delays except for her gross motor skills, like walking, and she was getting early interventions for that. She was playing, learning, speaking, and acting appropriately for her actual and corrected ages (the age she would have been if she had been born full-term).

Anyway, Imani didn't need to know about the medical details. She was busy doing her job of being a child. And I loved her unconditionally and I didn't focus on the tests. She was so excited to see her physical therapist, Kelly, and clapped her hands and giggled!

While we sat in the pediatric lobby waiting for Kelly, I read Imani the Dr. Seuss book *Oh, the Places You'll Go!* She loved when I read books to her and said, "Mom, make funny voices!"

Kelly appeared with her mouth wide open in a big smile. She wore a headband in her curly brown hair and had on khakis and a polo shirt. She was thin and athletic and high energy.

"Hi guys!" she exclaimed. "Don't you look fashionable today, Miss Imani! I love your bright colors!"

Kelly was a lot like Karen. She took an interest in our lives, and we talked through every therapy session. And also like Karen, she LOVED Imani. She talked about how she had wanted kids and it hadn't happened yet, so her therapy kids were her babies. For the past couple years, she had been praying to get pregnant. "It wasn't in God's Plan," she said with melancholy acceptance.

Her faith compelled her to do a lot to help people, and she shared stories of some of the community work that she was involved with. She was a very different Christian than the ones I knew. I thought about how some people had a smaller heart because of their religion, and some had a bigger heart and wanted to give their love to everyone.

"Let's try the stairs again," Kelly said. The physical therapy room had a lot of fun things, like a trampoline, short flights of stairs with railings, different sized steps, and different sized balls. Courage Center felt more like playtime than work to Imani, but she worked hard, nonetheless. Each week, she had three physical therapy sessions, when she did different exercises and stretches to loosen her tight muscles.

In between sessions, we practiced these activities several times per day using notes I took. And I bought her a small step and a tricycle, which Courage Center adapted for her, with longer foot pedals and straps to hold her feet in place. We added stickers she liked to the wheels to make riding even more exciting.

"Good job, Imani!" I praised her, as she planted her foot down on the step and pulled herself up by holding onto the railings.

"Me did it!" she said with determination, looking up at me with shining, happy eyes.

"Yes, you did, beautiful girl, yes, you did!"

"Me do it again!"

"You can do it!" I told her as I pointed to where she should grab on the railing.

She latched onto it and lifted her other leg, placing her foot halfway on the step.

"Almost there," I cheered.

A second time, she lifted her leg and pushed to place her foot completely on the step. A third time, a fourth, fifth, sixth, seventh…

"Mommy, me tired," Imani said in her cute little girl voice as she sat down on the last step.

"You did it! Your legs are getting stronger every day."

"I do stairs with Kelly."

"Yes, and you're going faster."

"Kelly is nice to me."

I remembered a particular preschool concert when Imani's class sang, "Each of us is a flower growing in life's garden; we need the sun and rain."

With Kelly and Karen and all the other nice people, we were not only surviving but thriving, and because of them, we had a chance. They were more of our string of paper suns.

Chapter 24: Girl for Sale

Josef is a man who does maintenance when I work on Saturdays at my security job during nursing school after high school graduation. He is fortyish and has long, black curly hair, which he wears in a ponytail. When I am at my desk, he spends a lot of time talking to me, and I respond politely.

"Have you ever had sex on the job?" he asks me, as though it is an ordinary question.

"No, I would never do something like that," I say. "Have you?"

"Oh yeah, sure. My wife and I have had sex upstairs. There aren't any cameras, and it's actually kind of a nice view of Minneapolis," he says.

"Oh, OK," I acknowledge, not sure how else to react.

"We have an open marriage," he goes on. "I think sex is natural, but people make it so taboo."

"I can see that," I muse. "I grew up in a church that was really strict about sex. I broke away from that."

"Good for you!" He applauds. "It feels good, and there's nothing wrong with it. People shouldn't be afraid to have sex. There are too many rules and everything. Why not live a little?"

Josef plunges his mop in the bucket and squeezes it out.

"You're shy, aren't you?" he inquires, clasping his hands over his mop.

I look at him without knowing what to say.

"You need to get out of your shell," he provokes. "Come on, let me show you the roof and some of the cool areas of this building."

"Well, I should do my rounds," I concede.

He leads me to the roof, and we rise out of the hatch on top to overlook the property and see the Minneapolis skyline in the distance.

"It's so pretty up here," he comments. "Do you like it?"

What if I let him touch me? Would I feel more alive? Maybe I am young and beautiful and need to have adventures. The women on the soap operas I had watched when I babysat at "unbelievers'" houses were passionate. I hate being so shy, and I wish I could be like other people. What Josef said made sense the more he talked.

"What are you thinking?" he invites, touching my shoulder.

"I'm cold up here," I retreat.

"Then we will come up here again when it gets warmer. I'll show you some other spots in this building that you might like, and they're warmer," he presses.

Josef leads me to some other office areas that I had already seen before, but he talks about them like he is a tour guide. Then we go into a small room that has a windowless door and a panoramic view of the outside.

"This is my favorite room." He approaches me. "I come up here when I need to think. It's private. I hope you like it, shy girl."

I laugh meekly. "I can see why you like it."

He chuckles. "There you go. Let loose a little. Let that personality out." His hand is rubbing my back. I say nothing.

Josef doesn't say anything either and gives me a back rub. His fingers drift to the back of my neck… then my face.

"You are really cute, you know that?" he compliments as he turns me around to face him. "If only I could get you to relax and be in the moment."

He leans his face toward mine and looks into my eyes, and I don't dare look away and come off as rude. "What are you thinking, beautiful?" he invites me again. And then he kisses me. I don't stop him; I don't want to upset him. He puts his hands on my waist and up and down my sides and moves to my breasts. He wants me to be fun like him. Everyone always told me that I needed to be more outgoing and more this and more that, and I hate disappointing people.

His dirty fingers open up my work shirt, and he pulls it off, so I am standing in front of him in my bra. And when I don't stop him, it is like another permission to go further. He massages my breasts like he is selecting grapefruit at the grocery store and kisses my nipples while he unhooks my bra. Throwing my bra on the floor, he puts his mouth on my bare tits and moans. "Your nipples are hard; I'm glad you finally loosened up, pretty girl."

Then as if to assume some sort of objectivity as he is molesting me, he holds my breasts in his hands and says, "I can tell that you've been pregnant before by your tits." His comment makes me feel slightly ugly, so it is almost like a favor that he is interested in me and my saggy tits.

I am like a sex doll, and he doesn't stop until after he has sex with me in several positions and cums on my tits.

Rigidly, I get up and escape to the bathroom to clean up and put my uniform back on. He takes me to other places in the building after that—and once to his van to have sex with me while he plays porno tapes he had made with his wife.

* * *

One day, when he isn't there, a patrol officer stops by. His name is Stephen. After talking to me at my desk for a while, he admits that he has always wanted to give a punk oral sex. I tell him that he can pay me $40 for fifteen minutes and we can do it in the bathroom.

Stephen leaves his car running outside, and we go into the ladies' room. I hold onto the frame of the bathroom stall and he holds me up on his shoulders with my legs dangling over his back. He devours me with his mouth and tongue and puts his fingers in me. When my timer goes off on my pager, I abruptly tell him that his time is up and he has to pay me.

Now I am in charge. I take back my power from all the men: the chef at the Holiday Inn who drove me to his house on lunch break and fucked me in his living room without a condom and had the nerve to ask me if he needed to get tested, the thirty-year-old former model from church, my lab partner in biology who got me wasted, puking drunk, and raped me in my car and left me to drown in my vomit, the man who drugged my drink at a friend's birthday party at a nightclub and drove me to an unknown apartment to rape me in front of his friends, and all the church guys who got me alone so they could put their hands up my shirt or down my pants. It's my game now, motherfuckers, I think. But I still don't know how to truly be powerful.

Chapter 25: Only God Knows

On a wintry Saturday in early February, Marcus was on good behavior, so I bent to his will and drove Imani to see him. Since the days of supervised visitation and their conclusion, Marcus had not followed through on the next step of family supervised visitation. Every time I talked to him about it, there was a heated argument and he refused to "let anyone control" him. Today, he had a calm demeanor and wasn't picking fights when we talked on the phone. I thought it would be an opportune time for him and Imani to bond with each other. As chaotic as Marcus had been with his death threats, abuse, and mind games, I wanted Imani to know her dad so she wouldn't feel abandoned. But he sure didn't make that easy.

"It's about time you got here!" he snarled when I got to his door with Imani and her bag.

I looked at my pretty, chubby-faced two-year-old little girl and hated to hand her over to this monster who was glaring at me. She meant more to me than life itself.

"Come on, are you going to just stand there?!" Marcus snapped at me. Like a switch had been flipped, he was back to being an ogre, but I didn't feel like I could back out without fueling the flames of his rage. I thought that if I did as he asked, his anger would be assuaged. It didn't feel like I could turn around now that we were already there.

Hugging Imani tighter, not wanting to let go, I tried to give her all of my energy and strength for whatever was ahead on this visit, not believing that he would actually hurt her. He hated me, not her. I kissed her on the cheek and held her out to Marcus. He snatched her away from me like he was claiming his rightful property and then grabbed Imani's bag off of my shoulder.

Inside the house where he was staying with his girlfriend, I saw him through the front window as he walked across the living room into the kitchen like he was marching. Timidly, I stood out of sight by the bushes and peered in to see if I could observe anything else. A minute later, he came back with a scowl on his face as he unzipped Imani's fleece coveralls and tossed them onto a chair that was piled with jackets. Again, he went back into the kitchen, but I couldn't hear any conversation. Afraid that he might catch me and get really mad, I snuck away to my car and drove off. My heart was pounding. But if I didn't let him have her at least occasionally, to placate him, I feared that he might try to take me back to court for full custody.

Driving down the road, I was unsettled, and it was hard to breathe. The pressure in my head was dialed up. I turned on the radio to try to ease my mind. Kid Rock was singing "Only God Knows Why" about finding yourself and karma and how you get what's coming to you. Then I switched the station and tuned into "Have You Ever Seen the Rain" by CCR—and I thought about all the pouring rain in my life and how it had to stop someday.

* * *

An hour later, I was back at my parents' house with all the familiar commotion and I sank into the recliner chair. But I couldn't relax. Mom asked me if I could help with the dishes now that I was back, but I was exhausted. She didn't push it. Within minutes, I was asleep.

* * *

Around 2:00 a.m., I woke up and realized that I had fallen asleep.

Marcus hadn't tried to call me at all, and this made me suspicious, but it was too late to call him. That would only spark a proverbial riot, and I wanted to keep everything copasetic for Imani.

I closed my eyes and tried to go back to sleep, but the silence was ringing in my ears and vibrating inside my head.

Is Imani asleep? Where is she sleeping? Was Marcus comforting to her at bedtime? Did she have enough to eat?

And there was nothing I could do.

The shadows moved across the kitchen with the moonlight. One of the kids got up to use the bathroom. Dad went into the kitchen for a drink of water. The night seemed to last for an eternity.

It was too easy to think too much. Two years had passed since Imani was born. It felt like a lifetime.

Only six months prior to her birth, I had been an eighteen year old coming home from work to an empty, lonely studio apartment in Minneapolis. My refrigerator had held a keg of stale beer, which I coveted, and a loaf of bread and the occasional frozen dinner from the Burch Pharmacy next door. And being on my own, back then, I thought I could finally be free and do whatever I wanted—including getting pregnant. Having a baby was a fantasy about being loved by a little creature who looked like me. But it was bullshit. My hormones and naïveté, along with years of trauma, had skewed my thinking. I was still a child without much life experience. It had been an emotional decision that was not carefully considered. My heart wanted what it wanted, and I leapt into motherhood with reckless abandon, hoping for the best—and in a state of denial, disregarding the worst that could happen. My guilt over my abortion was nothing compared to my guilt now. I had been ashamed only because the church treated it like murder, but it was my right and choice because it was my body. Of course, I loved my daughter, but I was way too young to become a mother when I had so much growing to do.

I had nothing except for the few belongings I had scraped together—toys, books, school stuff, and poetry I had written. Since leaving the church, I had lost all of my friends and hadn't replaced them yet—and didn't know how because I had never been allowed to make friends outside the church. My cousin told me that she couldn't be best friends anymore because I was an "unbeliever." It had been excruciatingly painful to leave my siblings behind because I felt responsible for them like a mother. I did not even have assets, or debt, because I hadn't gotten far in life yet to build a foundation, and already, I had lost everything I had known. Even my family was punished when I "gave up my faith"—especially when they went to "home services" in the neighborhood at homes of people I had babysat for. People questioned them and gossiped about me. Occasionally, I heard what people throughout the church were saying—that I was a wild girl, worldly, and a slut and drunk.

Having my own baby looked like having a life because it was akin to having a family and I would have someone to live for and take care of and bring with me everywhere. She would be my little best friend.

Without warning, though, my baby had been born fourteen weeks premature. I hadn't expected that, or anything else that followed. She had gone through more than I could imagine, and I was silly enough to think that I could give her a great life when I wasn't even stable enough for myself. And now she was at Marcus', and I had no control over what was happening.

Marcus had been a cute guy at the bar who had morphed into a person I could not have imagined—a sadistic misogynist who was also a lie that I believed in. Without scrutiny, I fell in love with what I wished he was and idealized him so he would fulfill my unmet needs and unrequited love. But he was sick and only took, took, took. Whatever he was in the mood for, he consumed. He made me responsible for his hatred of me and only loved me for what I could do for him and how powerful he could feel by trampling me. And he used our innocent child as a weapon against me.

People that I thought would help me didn't. Almost everyone who had been happy for me to become a mom disappeared. I knew they had their own lives, though, and it was folly to depend on them. Financially, I was drowning and unable to get by no matter how much I worked in my low-wage jobs. It was a vicious cycle of getting ahead a little bit and then being slammed backward. Every time I got up, I was kicked down.

Twice, I had moved out of my parents' house since initially being kicked out, and I ended up back there within a couple months. The first time I moved out was with a boyfriend who turned out to be a pimp and the second was to rent a closet in a farmhouse until the homeowner got wasted drunk and pounded on my door while I slept on the floor with Imani on a crib mattress.

There was always some drama to suck me dry. And I had set myself up for it all. *What would Tricia the social worker say about all of this?* She had told me that people make decisions based on life experiences that had shaped them. If I were to ask her if I was bad, she would say I wasn't and that I didn't know better at the time—but now I did. Her voice still rang in my ears: *"This happens to a lot of girls like you. Youth who don't have a strong support system are at-risk. I think it's also harder for you to read social cues and know when people are manipulating you."* I hoped she was right because I never meant to create such a mess.

My parents had really stepped up for Imani and me, after not being supportive until she was almost two years old. Letting me stay there for low rent, lending me money for my lawyer and bad checks, watching Imani for $2 per hour (plus interest). Plus, Imani had all of my brothers and sisters to play with and teach her. They were still strict about their house and expected me to generally follow their rules, and I went along with the program so we would have a home until we could afford to leave.

Mom's alarm clock went off. She was working a day shift at the hospital.

She came out into the living room and smiled at me. "Hi, sweetie."

"Hi, Mom," I whispered.

"You OK?" she asked as she paused at the kitchen doorway on her way to the coffee pot.

I sighed. "Marcus has Imani and I didn't hear anything from him last night," I replied.

"What a jerk," she said. "You don't treat a mother like that."

"Well, he has no decency, as you can see," I said, rubbing my eyes.

Mom finished getting ready, and I dozed off and on. When I couldn't sleep anymore, I got up and went through my notebook and picked at my to-do list. There was always so much I had to think about.

* * *

Marcus still hadn't called, and I checked my phone constantly. It was eleven o'clock; they had to be up by this time. So, I called.

"Hey, I'm wondering what time I should pick up Imani," I said, trying not to set him off. "How is she doing?"

"What the fuck is your problem? I hardly get to see Imani, and it hasn't even been twenty-four hours! You're such a selfish bitch!" he yelled. "And she's fine! So what if I did something to her? What could you even do about it?"

Worried that Imani would be scared if he got riled up, I tried to deescalate him. "No rush. I just wanted to know what you were thinking," I said softly.

"No! You can sit and wait for me like I always have to wait for you!" he yelled even louder.

"OK, OK. Will you call me this afternoon?" I asked, hoping we could set a time and keep it simple.

He hung up on me. I tried calling back and it went straight to voicemail. "Ugh!" I groaned and went outside for a cigarette.

Marcus called me back, and I answered immediately, hoping that he was going to be more reasonable. "Hi."

"You can pick her up in a couple hours," he promised. "But don't call me; I'll call you."

"OK."

Pacing in front of my parents' house, I smoked two cigarettes in a row even though it was bitterly cold and my hands were numb and I was shivering uncontrollably. My car was covered with a layer of fresh snow.

* * *

Two hours later, Marcus called me again. It was another two hours of fretting and pacing and smoking.

"Hi," I said, waiting for him to give me the green light to pick up Imani.

"It's going to be another couple hours. You know what, I don't even know! You're fucking ruining this whole time that I should be enjoying with MY daughter," he complained. A loud TV was on in the background.

"Marcus," I explained, "all I want to know is what the plan is, like what time I am picking her up. And also, I have to work tomorrow, so I have to get her today."

"I'll call you back," he said.

For another few hours, I waited. And waited. And waited. I went through a pack of cigarettes. And because I never felt like I could get started with my day because it was in limbo, I didn't even take a shower. I felt completely shut down. All I could focus on was getting Imani home. I tried to imagine what Imani was feeling and what was happening around her. Marcus had been violent toward me since I told him I was pregnant, and he had abused me throughout my pregnancy and since Imani's birth. But so far, I had not seen him direct anger at her. He had promised me that he would never hurt his own child, but he had also promised me he would be there for me. I felt sick not knowing what was happening and remembered Karen saying that there was a high risk that he would kidnap his child, so we had to take preventative measures, like not let him alone with her. My mind was racing, and my pulse was throbbing, and I tried to think good thoughts—that everything would turn out OK. But I wouldn't rest until my baby was back and I could check her for signs of whether Marcus had done something to her.

He called again and said that we could meet at the movie theater between us. Then he called and said that he would drive her out to my parents' house. And yet again, he didn't know what time. I lost track of how many times we spoke on the phone, but my cell phone knew: thirteen times. Every time, he extended the visit or changed the location to meet.

"Bridget, I'm going to keep her until Monday," he said. "I don't care if you have to work. You get to see Imani every day, and I have to wait around for you. I'll let you pick her up when I'm the one that's ready." All the alarm bells went off in my head at once, and I felt like I was going to lose it. Hours of holding in my worst fears and subduing my motherly instincts had come to a head. The time was continually being delayed, and it was starting to look like he might never bring her back. It was possible that he wasn't even in Minneapolis anymore and could be buying his time to kidnap Imani and take her far away. If I didn't act now, I could risk losing my baby!

"No, Marcus, you can't!" I cried. "You said I would get her back this afternoon and you've been playing this charade with me all afternoon! I'm getting her back tonight!"

A couple of my brothers questioned his behavior in the background, and Marcus heard them. "I'll put your entire family in the fucking hospital!" he threatened. Dad said that Marcus was not allowed on our property after that.

The phone calls went back and forth, and as hysterical as I was, I had to temper my reactions because Imani was in the middle of this horrific situation.

***

At 10:30 that night, I picked up Imani at Marcus' mother Delores' house, an hour from my parents'. I was so exhausted I could hardly see straight, and my nerves were shot. I felt like I was strung out from the constant adrenaline running through me.

A woman a few years older than me was sitting in the living room with a fat baby on her lap. Grandma Delores was holding Imani, and I practically pounced on her to fetch my beloved baby girl. I had no idea what she had been through for the last two days that were a never-ending nightmare for me. I couldn't stop snuggling her and kissing her plump little face.

"Who's the baby?" I asked, realizing that I didn't know who the mystery woman and child were.

Grandma Delores looked at me sheepishly. "That's Marcus' baby." She then introduced the mother, who looked at me bitterly. I had zero fucks to give to that situation, having been sufficiently ground down to the point that I was not going to take Marcus' drama anymore—at least for tonight.

Abruptly, I stood up and checked Imani's bag to see that she had everything since Marcus harvested what I sent, to keep at whatever place he was staying at for the time being. She was short one outfit and a sippy cup. At this point, I wasn't protesting something so small.

Imani started fussing and was restless. I tried everything I could think of: Worm Guy, songs, talking sweet to her. Nothing worked. She was inconsolable, and we didn't sleep until 1:00 a.m.

I thought about what the future would be like until Imani was eighteen years old and we could be emancipated from Marcus. I decided that the only way for us to survive was to avoid him. Until then, I would worry about dying and leaving Imani behind with him.

Chapter 26: Paper Suns

It is a hot summer day in Uptown Minneapolis in July 1997, and I am eighteen years old. My parents finally did what they had been threatening to do and kicked me out of the house for "giving up my faith" and being rebellious. The city is a whole new world to me—not only because it is a big city, but because I have never been immersed in mainstream society.

* * *

"If you don't stop sassing and wearing makeup in this house, you have to move out," my mom had demanded.

"Fine, you don't care what happens to me!" I had spewed, almost exploding from years of pent-up resentment and burnout. I had stormed downstairs toward my bedroom, making as much noise as possible as I stomped down the gold-carpeted stairs.

I had looked around the bedroom I shared with my sister, Claire, scanning it for what I wanted to take with me. I ripped everything off the hangers and stuffed it into a duffel bag. I packed my dark blue Oldsmobile with as much as I could, especially what I would need in the coming weeks. There was no time to pack with any intention. I was out of there!

Fired up, I tore down the road, away from all that bound me. Lighting a cigarette, I cranked Bryan Adams on a cassette mix tape I recorded from the radio. It was forbidden music in the church, but I didn't go there anymore.

* * *

After living with an older boyfriend for a month, I got my own apartment on the second floor of the Belmont on Hennepin and Franklin.

A white ledge runs the length of the windowsill, and that's where I sit and keep my ashtrays. It's where I smoke cigarettes and watch people and traffic, and gaze at the Minneapolis skyline. Where I watch ballet classes in the studio across the street because I always wanted to dance. It is the place I go to imagine being somewhere else, as though my windows offer a portal to any place I can dream of.

Over the summer, I dump my mail into one of the lower cupboards of a built-in dresser near the bathroom and neglect it in favor of beer, making new friends, and exploring without restrictions or parental complaints. On the top, I place things that I like to look at—the remains of my abbreviated childhood: my Little Bo Peep porcelain doll, a thick plastic Cabbage Patch Doll piggy bank, doilies that I collected, perfume bottles (some empty), a porcelain Cinderella figurine that I got from Disneyland when I was five, a wooden frame that my great-grandfather had made (without a picture), a few textbooks that I couldn't bear to sell back to my college at the end of the semester, and a rough draft of a poem I wrote from the heart.

As I get settled into my new home, it is eerily quiet after coming from a home filled with people.

Nobody calls me or visits. I'm not sure I want anyone to. And my boyfriend and I have broken up because I don't know if I love him anymore.

When I want to shut out the world, I slide the windows down, unhook the shutters, and bring them together, chasing the light away and enclosing myself in the darkness and quiet, and calm, where I can't be found—sometimes even by myself.

When I am lonely, I look at the string of paper suns I've taped along my ceiling and their little smiley faces and I feel like I have company. Sometimes I even talk to them about my day, and they never stop smiling at me. They feel like friends.

As soon as I get off work, I change into shorts and a tank top, put on my eyeliner and lipstick, and walk across the street to my watering hole "Liquor Lyle's," which is like a punk/retro/urban dive bar version of "Cheers." The local folks hang out here, and I get to know and become one of the regulars. If I get there early enough, I can get in before the bouncers are at the doors. Then they don't card me at the bar for the rest of the night.

Warmth flows through my body as the humid air kisses my taut, tan skin. After a couple beers, my breathing relaxes and my thoughts slow. My friends are laughing around the bar, and I am smiling at everyone with my dark outlined lipstick, white teeth, and a sense that life is nearing perfection. Everyone seems to be my friend who is there to talk to, confide in, and savor. When our favorite songs come on the jukebox, we shriek in shared recognition and sing along—sometimes using our beer bottles as pretend microphones. A cloud of our collective and constant cigarette smoke hangs around us. Into the early morning hours, we carouse and feel on top of the world, as if nothing can touch us. "I love you all!" I think. Surely, they feel the same way about me. For the first time, I feel included.

While sipping on a beer at Liquor Lyle's, a tall, ripped guy oozing with confidence and wearing a baseball cap beams at me.

"Hey," I say with a brief wave and a demure glance that says I am clearly interested but want him to make the first move.

"Did it hurt when you pierced your nose?" he asks.

"Not bad; I actually did it myself with a piercing kit," I reply coolly, sliding the piercing.

"I pierced my nipple and I had to take it out," he discloses.

"That seems like it would be a lot more painful," I flatter him.

"I'm Marcus, and I approve of your piercing." He chuckles, extending his hand to shake mine. It is a strong, manly hand, which I imagine all over my body.

"I'm Bridget, and accept your approval," I tease. We talk about what we've been doing over the summer.

"Do you want to meet my cats?" I ask Marcus, making the excuse that I forgot to feed them.

"Well, I'm allergic, but I'll stop by," he agrees, his face conveying that he is clearly more enthusiastic than that.

We walk across the street to my apartment, and I give him a beer. We talk about things we dream about doing one day. He wants to start his own business and have a family. I plan to go back to college and become a scientist. We hook up a few times and think we're in love—although we never go on a proper date.

* * *

The sun comes up fast after these nights. Possibly still partly drunk, I squint at my alarm clock. It is after 10:00 a.m., and I have to be at work by 1:00 p.m. My cats, Freya and Venus, are in bed with me, playing with each other. They are my backup alarm clock. Rustling around in my king-sized pink comforter with large tulips, I stick my feet out and close my eyes. It is a bed that I bought with my babysitting money several years ago, from an ad in the newspaper. I roll over again and the cats jump off. My head is spinning, but I have to get up.

Sitting up, I look out my row of long windows at Minneapolis, which is already well into the work day, stretching forward toward the chipped green polish on my toes. Leaning back, I look in my headboard mirror at my makeup-smeared face. What time had I even gone to bed? I wonder.

* * *

That night, I am back at Lyle's again. I swing open the bathroom stall door, which doesn't lock, and watch myself approach the mirror where another girl is fixing her ponytail. She has bright blue hair and short bangs. Trying not to look like a creeper for staring at her, I peek at her and then look down at my pockets as I fish for my lipstick. In the church, I hadn't been around people like her up close. Church people would have thought she looked like a prostitute, but I am fascinated by her exotic style and enamored of her. I wind up my maroon lipstick and put it on, and then play with my hair to extend my time next to this creature. "Hi," she says.

"Hi," I reply. She walks out, and I linger in front of the mirror at the new Bridget I see—a free bird with makeup on and a nose ring and hoop earrings, and I fluff my hair again. I wonder what my family is doing right now and if they're thinking of me. With all my glorious liberty, I'm sad for them because their lives seem so boring and claustrophobic. As I push open the bathroom door, the sound of the jukebox escalates, and I go back to the bar where I have been flirting with a group of guys and girls.

Bar closes, and it is 1:00 a.m. on a clear summer night with a few visible stars in the city sky. I am walking through an Uptown neighborhood with a few friends from the bar, on our way to an after-party at some random guy's house. He said he had more booze and some pot. I am wearing short cut-off jean shorts and a black knit button-down shirt with a white collar and a necklace made of horseshoe nails. My lipstick and ID are in one pocket, and my cigs and lighter are in the other. I had spent all my cash, but a few guys had bought me drinks. Life is so fun and whimsical, and I have the perfect buzz. My new friends are talking about going to Hidden Beach the next weekend and invite me to go along. It is a secluded spot where you can go topless. I wink at one of the guys, and he puts his arm around me. When we get to the party, he stays by my side. We sneak away to an upstairs bedroom while everyone is sharing a bong and have sex without a condom because neither of us has one. He walks me home sometime after 5:30 in the morning when the sun is starting to peek over the horizon.

* * *

A few nights later, after eating a few pieces of beer-smelling bread that is about the only food in my refrigerator, I venture downtown to the Gay 90s by myself, wearing my purple club wig.

Downtown is very busy, and I park my blue 1989 Oldsmobile in a parking ramp about a half a mile away from the Gay 90s. Looking in the rearview mirror, I straighten my wig and add another application of plum lipstick. My eyes pop when I wear this wig, especially with the cat-eye makeup.

When I get out of the car, I push the upright peg lock down on the door and shut it. My night is about to begin.

A drag queen with long, fire red hair glides toward me from the other direction and announces, "Hey, gorgeous, I LOVE your hair." I smirk and keep strutting. A drunk man is playing Bob Dylan on a guitar with a donation can at his feet. A sad-faced woman is selling roses.

There is a short line when I get to the Gay 90s, and I double-check that I still have my ID and cover charge; I probably don't need drink money since I am fully loaded. As I enter the club, I am met with the flashing lights, pounding bass, and the glow of colorful people who are mingling at the bar, grooving on the dance floor, and looking chic holding a drink while watching everyone else. That night, I go home with a guy and a chick, because I can.

Singing church songs in my rocking chair

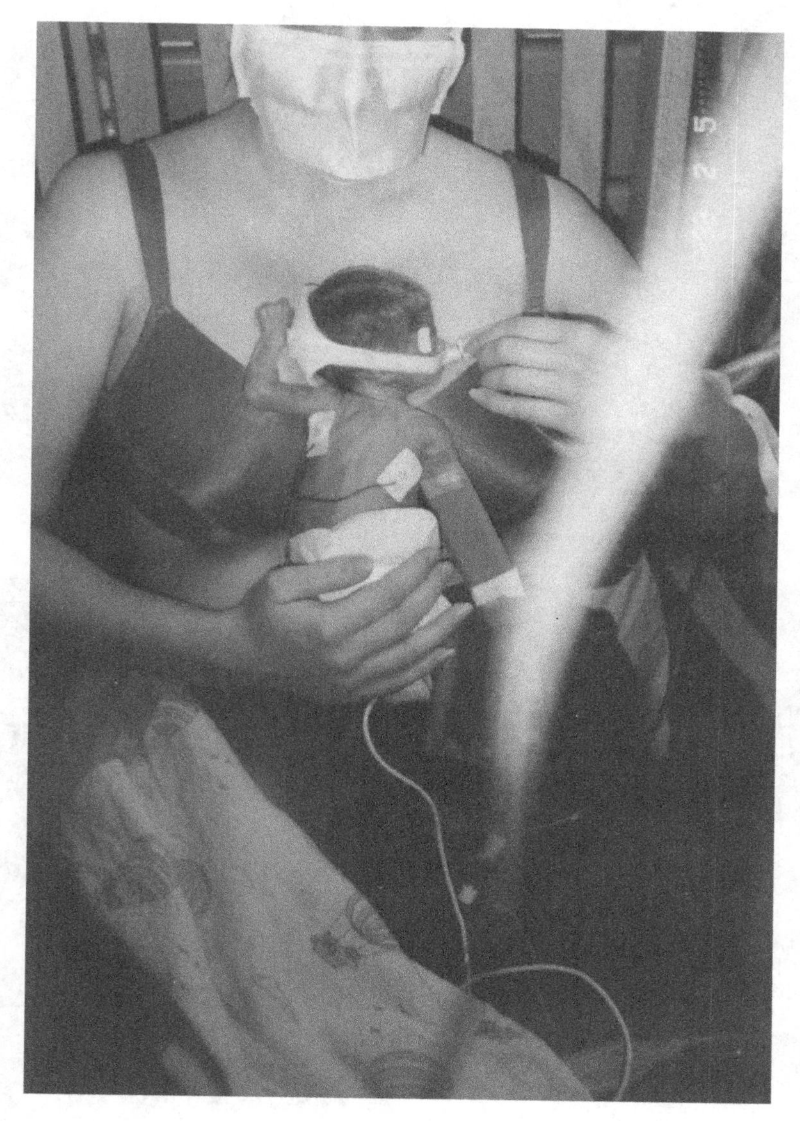

Kangaroo care when Imani was five days old

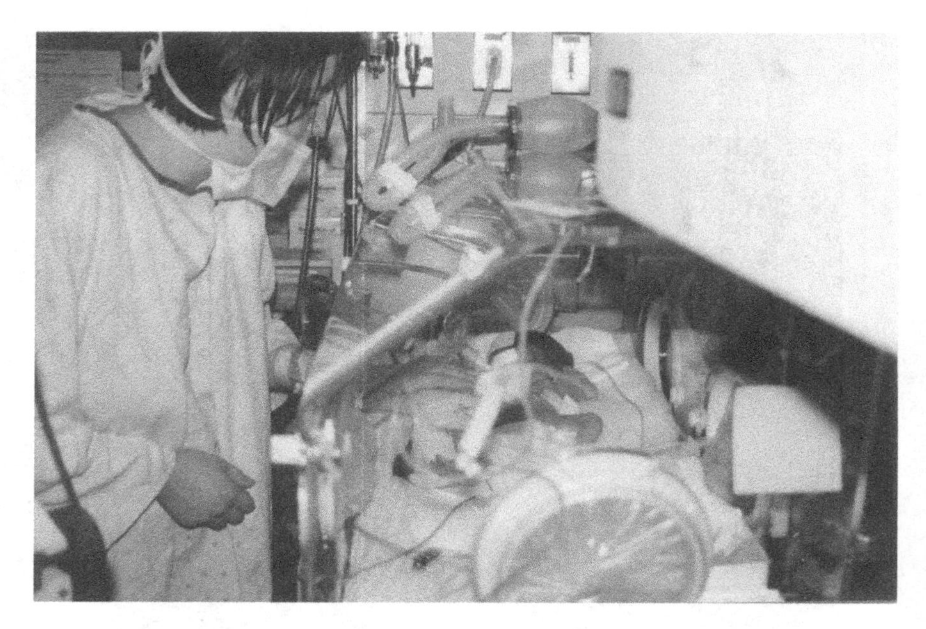

In awe of my daughter's beauty when I meet her

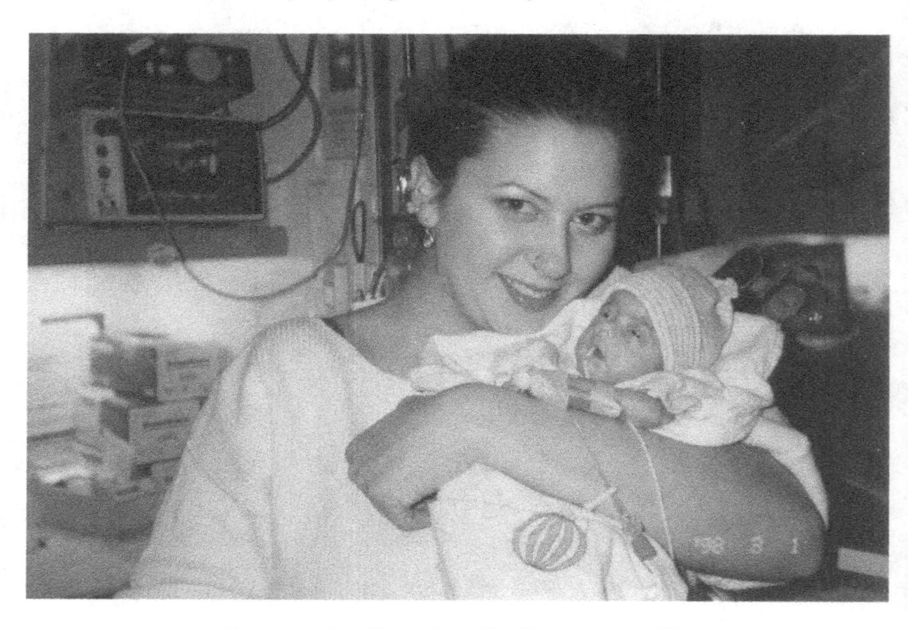

One month old, and we finally get to cuddle

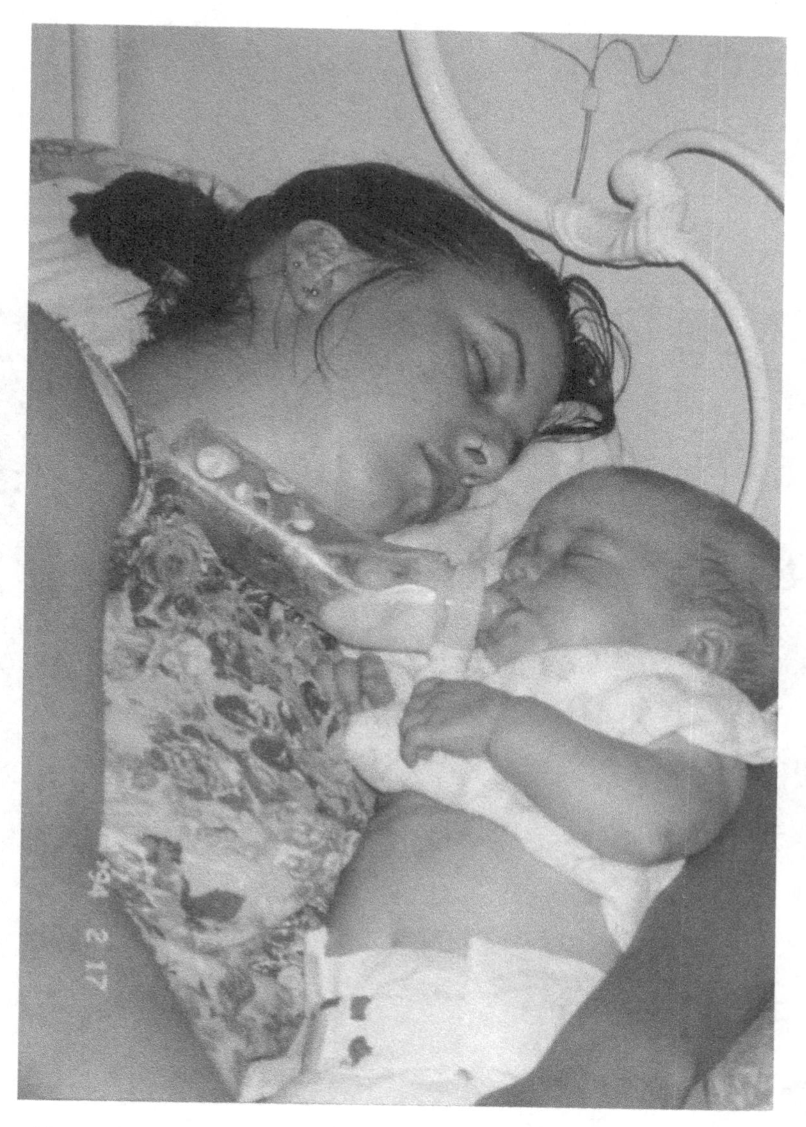

Even when we're sleeping you can see the pure love (incorrect date)

All I see is you (incorrect date)

What happens when three young women want their princess to have the best Christmas ever (incorrect date)

I could snuggle my baby in my arms all day (incorrect date)

My little comedian

Hanging out at Grandma and Grandpa's

Imani, you are my shining star

Holiday greeting photo of us playing at the park

Our first apartment of our own

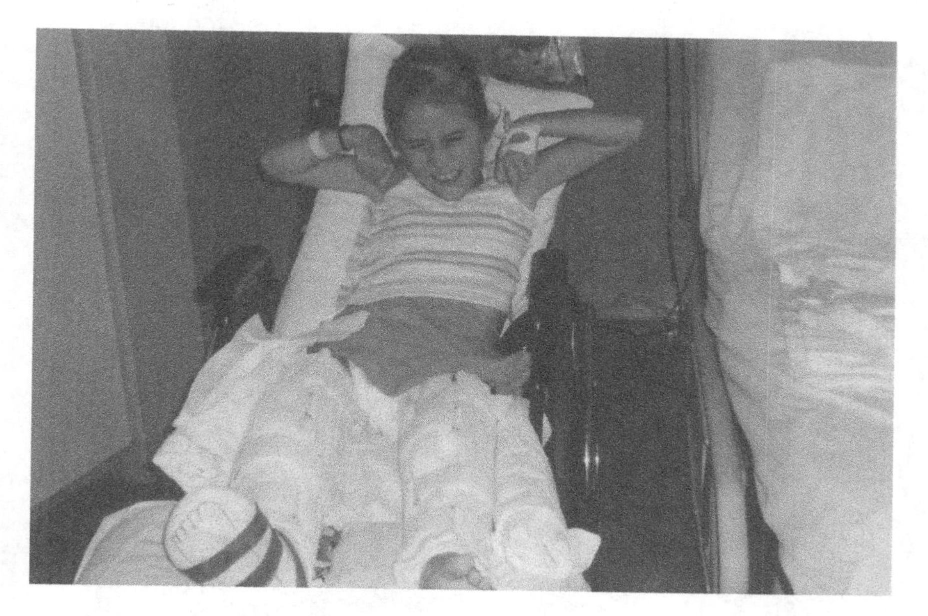

First surgery shenanigans

Always so much fun with you

My first time in Washington, DC; meeting with congress on Capitol Hill

Chapter 27: Old Home Week

Pulling my baby-blue 1994 Topaz into the parking lot on a crisp autumn morning, I scanned my potential new home. It was across the street from the Klapprich Park & Field, where I had gone sledding and ice-skating with my cousins as a girl. We had biked into Wayzata during the summers, and the nostalgia was comforting. I wanted to raise Imani in the Wayzata School District because it was one of the best in the country. A lot of the same stores were still there, and for a thriving community, not much had changed. I turned off my cassette tape player and unbuckled my seat belt. The building was old brown brick with a worn Mansard-style roof and chipped wrought iron balconies, and it was what we needed. Jennifer from the management office was already there to greet me for my tour.

"Hi, did you have any trouble finding it?" she asked me.

"No, I knew this area already. Do people still ice-skate at the park?" I responded.

"Yeah, I think the rink gets flooded around November, and the warming houses are staffed in December sometime," she told me.

Remembering putting on my ice skates, over a double layer of socks, in the warming house with my friends made me feel right at home. It would be a good place to bring up a child. I could give her the best of my world and what I had never had. This would be the place that I could get a do-over of my own childhood, vicariously through my daughter. She would get to do all the things I had missed out on, and somehow that would make it right. I would let her play with any friends she wanted to, join sports and band, and go to school dances. She would listen to whatever music she wanted and see movies with her friends. I would never make her friends clean our home and would let them stay up late, eating popcorn and laughing. When her friends had problems at home, my daughter could tell them proudly that they could talk to me and I wouldn't judge them. In this old familiar place, I was going to recreate a life that I thought had passed me by.

"Do you want to see the one-bedroom?" Jennifer asked me.

"Absolutely," I replied as I turned around to face the entrance of the two-story building that was partly covered in vines.

"If you like it, we can go back to the rental office to do an application. We're going to look at 107," she offered, as though she was confident in renting to me.

Jennifer unlocked the door and led me into the apartment on the first floor. There was a spacious coat closet with room for storage to the left in the entry, which faced a living room straight ahead, with a kitchen to the right and a hallway leading to a bathroom and bedroom on the left. Across the beige-carpeted living room, my eyes were drawn to the back yard off the small slab of concrete patio. My mind placed a kiddy swimming pool and tricycle and pot of flowers in the new backdrop of my life as an independent woman and mother. We went into the bedroom, which had a window and another closet. We could have our own space with all of our things in one place.

"This will definitely work!" I said, pleased.

* * *

That evening when I went back to Cubby's for my 6:30 p.m. to 8:30 p.m. shift, I told him all about the apartment.

"Good for you, Bridge. I think it sounds right for you and Imani," Cubby said enthusiastically.

I thanked Cubby and told him that it was $750 per month. Then I asked if I could ever bring Imani with me to work in the evenings so I wouldn't have to drive back to my parents' house every night for a two-hour shift. Otherwise, I would have to drive to and from my parents' and Cubby's twice a day, which would be a lot of miles and hours—and hardly worth it.

"For me, that would be fine, but I don't think that Gigi would allow it. She's very particular about her home," he said.

"Would you mind asking her?"

Gigi called from the kitchen, "Dinner is almost ready, so Cubby needs to be up in his wheelchair in about five minutes!"

I got the urinal from the laundry room adjacent to the living room and Cubby "took a leak," as he called it. Then I dumped and rinsed it in the bathroom in the front entry of their townhouse and walked back, passing the kitchen.

Again, Gigi instructed me to get Cubby up quickly because dinner was about to be served. Rushing, I put the urinal back and moved his wheelchair hurriedly next to his bed. We did the transfer as we did about sixty times per month: raised the head of the bed, swung his legs over the side of the bed, pulled his torso up so he was in a sitting position, and stood him up into a pivot transfer that turned him 45 degrees into a sitting positing in his wheelchair, parallel to the position he had been in in bed.

"You're so smooth," Cubby praised me.

"It's like a dance," I said, doing jazz hands. I loved how we worked together so gracefully. He didn't bark orders at me like some had. Cubby asked me to do things in the form of a question. "Will you change the channel?" "Will you pull my butt back?" "Will you raise the head of the bed?" With him, I was not subservient. Feeling appreciated, I was compelled to do everything I could for him. Whether I was at home or went out with him, I wanted to make things perfect. That was especially difficult in public when we encountered more barriers, like small bathrooms, few safe places to transfer, negative attitudes about disability, and crowds we couldn't get through. Sometimes even clinics and hospitals, where he went for appointments, were inaccessible. There were rooms that weren't big enough, exam tables that weren't low enough, and a couple times, there wasn't the necessary lift equipment to get him into an MRI machine; I had to hoist him up and hope that I didn't drop him.

"Cubby and Bridget, I'm waiting!" Gigi yelled from the kitchen. Surely she had not instilled the dignity in her son; he must have gained it elsewhere.

Quickly, I put on Cubby's foot pedals and rolled him into the kitchen. It smelled good, and I hadn't had time for dinner. Gigi had baked meatloaf into green peppers and covered them with a red sauce and toasted a loaf of garlic bread. As I pushed Cubby into his spot at the table and put his brakes on, she poured him a beer into a glass he had gotten while traveling in Germany. Her glass of wine was already refilled and full.

"Yum, this looks great, Gigi," I complimented her. I longed for warm sustenance.

"Well, I like to make a home-cooked meal. It's terrible that people eat so much microwaved and fast food. I hope you cook for your daughter." Her whole face scowled at me with arrogance. She had never seen the depths of my existence. Her vantage point was an assumed moral high ground.

"I don't have time, but maybe one day I will," I said, equally embarrassed and indignant, though trying to feign diplomacy. After all, I was preoccupied with their dinner and I couldn't be in two places at one time. I put on Cubby's apron and adjusted his arms.

Gigi squinted at me. "You should give your daughter a proper diet."

"I'm not home during dinner, so she usually eats at my parents' house and has whatever they're having. She gets good meals," I said in my defense.

"That's nice, but that's no way to bring up a child," Gigi said, penetrating me with her callous regard for what she presumed about my life out of ignorance.

"Mother!" Cubby interrupted, straining to raise his voice.

"Feed Cubby his dinner before it gets cold," she ordered.

My stomach growled as I cut up Cubby's food and fed him in between giving him swigs of his beer with a flexible straw. Gigi went on a rant, as she drank her wine, about how she felt about the disintegration of the nuclear family and how mothers didn't stay at home like they did in her day. I heard only part of it through my hunger and focus on my job. Each morsel of food I delivered with care was a kick in my stomach, and each sip of a drink was a reminder that I was poor.

After dinner, Cubby wanted to watch a football game on television and asked me to do his range-of-motion exercises. I did passive range-of-motion on him that I had learned in nursing school: raising his arms into a stretch and holding it, raising his elbows, raising his forearms, and stretching his wrists. Each stretch was specific to a muscle or group of muscles. Since he couldn't move, his muscles had atrophied and become small and weak. Nevertheless, he reminisced about the times he played golf and committed himself to staying in the best shape he could so he could return to it after he got the "magic bullet" from his doctor at the Mayo Clinic.

He loved watching football, especially the Vikings. Gigi told stories about wearing her mink coat to the outdoor stadium and drinking wine with other fancy socialite women.

***

One week I had taken him to a game. Along with the usual morning routine of getting out of bed, breakfast, shower, hair, teeth, clothes, we packed a few things for the day: urinal, disability parking tag, pills, straws, wallet, and tissues. Gigi made Belgian waffles on game days—to be festive and give Cubby a big meal to hold him over. Then I pushed Cubby to the garage to transfer him into the car using a pivot transfer again, and disassembled his wheelchair, and put it in the trunk.

The stadium was booming loud and disorienting with all the sounds, lights, and people. There was a steep incline on the way up to the Metrodome. After helping Cubby get through security for people in wheelchairs, I pushed him, per his lead, to the section on the second tier. His seats were the first two on the bottom row, the only row with easy access.

During halftime, I took him to the bathroom and had to endure the "locker room talk" of the men's room because there were no family or accessible restrooms. Several men laughed at their dirty jokes at our expense and made comments like, "I'm next!" through the door. I tried not to tell them to go fuck themselves as I rinsed out the urinal and washed my hands.

* * *

Tonight they were playing in Philadelphia, and I was in Cubby's living room—a quieter, less misogynist atmosphere.

"OK, Bridge, you can get me ready for bed," Cubby said at 7:45.

"What sleep shirt do you want?"

"How about the college one?"

It was from his alma mater—he referred to college as "the best four years of my life." I heard many college stories and then the trajectory of his career following: teaching in a private boarding school, then another, and then being recruited into fundraising and development. His last campaign was 650 million dollars, and he was still proud of how much good it did for students and the world. There was no question that he was one of "the good old boys," but he used his privilege to elevate as many people as possible. His college shirt was a ratty T-shirt, and he liked them that way. He called them "Survivor shirts," in reference to the TV show *Survivor*. One day we would go on the show, he would say. And, of course, win.

Like every night, we did the bedtime routine: sleep shirt, brush teeth, wash face, put on creams, and take pills. In the bathroom, I put toothpaste on his toothbrush and filled his water cup with a straw and gathered the small hand towel for his mouth and tray to spit in. Then I returned to the bathroom to clean up everything and went to the laundry room to wet a washcloth in hot water to wash his face. I then applied a variety of creams a dermatologist had prescribed for him to help stop the neurological itching that plagued him. As I raised the head of Cubby's hospital bed, I yawned.

"You've had a big day. Go home and get some sleep," he said, relieving me from duty.

"I will after I pick up Imani and take her home. We usually get home by ten," I said, tired just thinking about it.

"Sleep fast."

Chapter 28: Who's Your Daddy?

"Imani, do you want to go see Daddy?" I asked her as she worked intently on her bowl of ice cream and pushed her messy hair out of her face with the less sticky back of her hand. My brother, Trevor, who was six months older, sat on the table with his bowl of ice cream and was laughing at my youngest brother, Brian, who was hamming it up—obviously with a sugar rush in full swing. Imani didn't seem to hear me, as she was engrossed in the much more interesting antics of her two uncles.

"Huh?" She looked up at me, quizzically.

"Do you remember Daddy? He wears a white hat. We saw him at Grandma Delores' house, and your sister was there," I reminded her. Marcus was behaving again, and I thought he seemed to be in a better place. This was a chance to build on that and try to create a healthier future for Imani with her dad in her life.

"Daddy called me a baby," she said, taking another bite of ice cream and laughing at Trevor and Brian.

"Yes, he did, because you are his baby and he loves you," I said. "Daddy misses you and wants to see you."

"I don't wanna go there. I'm playing with Tweh-voh and Bwy-in!" she insisted as Trevor and Brian zoomed back and forth and wrestled with each other.

She had ice cream all over her face and was clapping her hands as she giggled. My dad came into the kitchen and started playing guitar—folk music with a catchy twang. Imani started bobbing her head to the rhythm and blurting out belly laughs. My parents had loosened up over the past several years as the siblings who followed me got older. Apparently, I had broken them in.

Dad chuckled at Imani and played faster to encourage her. Down from the table she went and started her signature bouncing dance. It was contagious, and we all danced along, with slight reservation, even though the church did not allow dancing.

I had to break up the party to make Marcus happy. He was rarely present, but when he did show up, I became submissive to him. I had grown up in patriarchy—obeying men and male figures. It was automatic by this point.

* * *

"You're getting so big!" Marcus said as he picked up Imani and turned his head to shoot me a dirty look as if to insinuate that she had grown up without him. He marched off with her with authority into his building and up the stairs to his apartment, and I followed.

Inside his apartment there was a sofa in the middle of the room with clothes strewn on it. A dirty plate sat on the TV stand, and there were papers and miscellaneous things on the floor.

Marcus put Imani down on the sofa and pulled me onto his lap. "Come here, slut. You look good. Why do you have to be so difficult?"

He was tall and built like the amateur football player that he was, had a million-dollar smile and a swagger that made all the girls swoon. Even though I was afraid of him, I was drawn to his bravado and the bad boy façade. I wanted to gain his approval by loving him enough. It was like being with a dark, twisted version of a homecoming king—one who was exciting but made my life a living hell.

"Go take a quick shower," he ordered. "I don't need no stinky pussy and I know your hippie ass don't clean."

There were no washcloths in his bathroom, so I washed up the best I could by lathering soap on my hands. He must have heard when I was done because he opened the bathroom door as I was drying off. "Look at those titties. Can you still spray milk for me?" he said, licking his lips.

"Where is Imani?" I asked, worried about leaving her alone and not wanting to be apart from her for long.

"Will you calm down? Oh my God, you're so nervous about everything! I put in a movie, and she's glued to the TV," he said.

"Well, we shouldn't be doing this. I just came over here to let you see her for a while before bedtime," I said.

He rolled his eyes. "You have to make such a big deal about everything. She's not gonna die if she stays up for an extra hour. Now get in the bedroom because you're wasting more time with your yapping."

Obediently, I went into his bedroom, which was an even bigger mess than the living room, with his clothes everywhere and a pair of panties on the nightstand.

"Lie down and take off that stupid towel already. Geez, did you become a nun or something?" he sneered as he pulled the towel off of me and pushed me onto his bed and got on top of me, his penis already hard.

He grabbed my vagina and put his fingers inside me, "Yeah, you need some of this; lemme brush off the cobwebs." He took over and knew he could get away with it as he had so many other times.

For the next half hour, he pushed and pulled my body to where he wanted it like he was ravaging a chunk of red meat on an empty stomach. Every few minutes, he grabbed a towel that had been on the floor to wipe his face as the sweat dripped onto me. I lay there waiting for it to end so I could put my clothes back on. Shame flooded my veins.

Back in the living room, Imani was still watching TV and didn't seem to be aware of anything beyond her show. Marcus tried to kiss me like he was marking his territory, and I pulled back. It didn't feel right to let Imani see us being lovey-dovey when we weren't together. After all he had done to me, my heart still ached to be with him. But he didn't appreciate or respect me.

"Cold already?" he said, slapping me across the face.

"Marcus, you will never be happy with what I give you, and you just take, take, take. Like how much money do you even owe me?" I reminded him as I recalled the times I had helped him, incensed by my stinging cheek.

"I don't owe you shit!" he shot back.

I reminded him of the many times I had bailed him out financially when he had gone to jail or his vehicle was impounded, and raising my voice, I demanded that he pay me back and consider the thousands he owed me in back child support.

Marcus started pushing me, and I put my arms up to block him. He grabbed my arms tightly so I couldn't fight him, but I wriggled to free myself.

"You're just making it harder for yourself," Marcus warned me. "Keep trying, and I'll fucking choke you!"

Imani's show was still on, but she wasn't watching it anymore; she was standing in the doorway, her face puckered up into a look of fright, and she began to cry.

"Marcus, let me go! Imani's crying and she shouldn't be seeing this!" I pleaded with him.

"Shut up! This is your fault because you always have to start shit. You always motherfucking start shit and act so perfect!" He held my arms tighter and pushed me around. Continuing to fight to loosen his grip and try to talk to Imani only further enraged him, and he pushed me down onto the floor and grabbed me around the throat. I couldn't breathe or talk as he held me down and I panicked. With all of my strength, I was able to turn myself sideways so he couldn't push his body weight onto my neck. He was too big and strong for me—I was no match for him. Somehow, I was able to get onto my stomach, and then my phone started ringing.

"My family is expecting me back already—let me go!" I yelled, competing with Imani's cries. She had picked up her doll and was sitting by the door, heaving as she waited for me.

The phone call threw him off, and he stood up, even more furious. Before the violence could escalate further, I ran toward Imani, snatching my purse off the couch, and whisked her out the door. Marcus yelled behind me, but I didn't process what he was saying because it happened so fast. Next thing I knew, I was outside running to my car with Imani in my arms. Full of adrenaline, I was trembling too much to put her into her car seat, so I sat her on the back seat and jumped into the driver's seat. I was shaking like a leaf as I dialed 911.

"911, what's your emergency?"

"My daughter's father tried to kill me!" I shrieked as I tried not to drop the phone. "She's with me!" Imani was sobbing in the back seat, her little traumatized face looking wide-eyed everywhere at every sound and sight.

Two police officers arrived a few minutes later and spoke with me. They took photos of the marks on my neck and went into Marcus' building. I wasn't sure how long they were gone because my mind was going 100 miles an hour, but everything still felt like slow motion. One of the officers came back and said that they had arrested him and I was free to go.

Driving down the road back to my parents' house, I was relieved to be out safely with Imani, but I grappled with heavy guilt over what Imani had been through and remorse about taking her to see him when he had been so aggressive earlier. I told myself that there was no way that I would let that happen again.

"Imani, you're my princess, and I love you," I tried to console her. "Daddy was naughty and he was being mean to you and mommy." It horrified me that she could learn that this was normal and grow up to be in these kinds of situations.

"Daddy mean," she repeated.

That night, after getting back to my parents' quiet, sleeping house, I snuggled with Imani and told her how special she was and what a wonderful girl she was.

"I love you, Imani. I will always love you and be nice to you," I reassured her.

"Thank you for loving me," she said, turning toward me and kissing me on the cheek. I hugged her tighter and we drifted off to sleep.

Marcus was charged with fifth-degree domestic assault, interference with an emergency call, disorderly conduct, and damage to property. He pled guilty to lesser charges.

Chapter 29: Tiptoe Away

"Bridget, come here, will you?" Gigi said. She shuffled through her morning newspaper that she always read with a cup of coffee while she waited for the aide to show up. Then she folded the paper to show me something, which she often did.

"Is this the roommate you've talked about?" she asked, drawing my attention to an article.

It was Jessica's obituary.

It had her picture, so there was no denying that it was her: the familiar radiant smile, blonde hair shining in the sun, and twinkling eyes that saw all the good in the world with a perpetual innocence that defied the hell she had been through. The last time I had seen her was when Valerie kicked her out of our Foley apartment and I didn't fight for her to stay because I couldn't handle one more crisis. So, she left, and I never saw her again.

"I wonder what happened to her," I said, looking up at Gigi, yearning for elderly wisdom.

"For a young woman to die at twenty-four years old, it can't be good."

She snipped the obituary out of the newspaper and handed it to me, and I put it in my purse. "Do you mind if I have a cigarette before I get Cubby up?" I asked.

"Not at all," Gigi replied. "You take all the time you need, but just get him up by eleven."

I stood in their driveway and went through three cigarettes as my memories of Jessica flashed through my mind: her hollering at me from the street to come up when I had my studio apartment in Minneapolis, all the times she made food for me when I was pregnant, us fighting over bills, her driving me to the hospital when I was in labor, moving with her to her nasty mom's house and living locked in rooms, our escape to the Foley apartment and her mom reporting us for burglary (for taking our own stuff with us), when she reassured me after my car accident on my way home from a long day of work, living on potatoes and the food shelf, how she enjoyed taking Imani on stroller rides when she took her walks… I should have known somehow, intuitively, that my dear friend was in trouble. And yet, she tiptoed away.

I crushed out my last cigarette and put it on the patio by the front door next to the cement angel and went inside. A loving God wouldn't have let this happen. He was as cold as the cement angel.

"Hey, Cubby," I said as I rested my right arm on his bed, next to him. "Gigi showed me my roommate Jessica's obituary, and I went out for a couple cigs."

"She told me. It's OK, Bridge," he said sympathetically. "I've lost friends and I know it's very, very tough."

His kind words were like permission to feel my grief, and I stood at his bed and wept. He turned his attention back to the show he was watching and gave me space for a few minutes.

I nearly yelled, "Cubby, she was so young…and beautiful… It's not fair!"

"You're right," he replied, stiffening with a sudden yawn that brought on a spasm, which threw his left leg off the side of the bed. "Life can be cruel." He often told me that when he woke up in the morning, he was angry at first when he realized his condition. But that he then settled into his day. When I calmed down, I got Cubby up for the day.

* * *

Since I had a wink of time and was on state healthcare, I made an appointment to get a physical and pap smear.

I couldn't remember who my primary doctor was because I couldn't even remember when I had last been to the doctor. Cubby went to a health campus that had many providers, so I called them and made an appointment with a nurse practitioner. I was afraid of cancer and leaving Imani behind with Marcus.

Sitting in the waiting room, I was nervous because I was afraid of what might be found in my physical and I didn't want to talk about my drinking and smoking. Although I knew that as soon as I left, I would probably be back to my habits.

I picked up a magazine and read about the latest in Hollywood, wondering what it would be like to have what you need, plus extra. My whole life had been a battle to survive. Growing up, we had to get government help for food, and we drove cars that broke down constantly, and Dad had to spend all his time fixing. Once he blurted out, "I hate fixing cars!" and that surprised me because he was usually mellow and passive.

My dad with his easy swagger and shaggy haircut that he whipped out of his eyes, and his handsome good looks, artist soul, and dreams of becoming a college professor. My mom, once with her angelic face and petite figure, her feathered brown hair that was like from a magazine (like the one I was reading), Fifth Avenue perfume, and short heels because the church was against anything sexy. Her amazing talent as an artist stopped with her last painting after the first couple kids. Life had changed them. Now when I saw them, they were tired and overwhelmed.

"Bridget!" I put the magazine down and went into the exam room and put my purse down on the spare chair.

The nurse asked me questions about my health history and lifestyle. I admitted to smoking and underestimated how much I drank, saying it was two to three drinks per day.

When the nurse practitioner came in, she reviewed my information and asked me what I did for work. I told her that I was a caregiver, but that I was going to college.

"Fantastic! And what are you hoping to do after college?" she asked.

"I think I want to go to grad school to become a therapist," I said. "But I need time to recover after I finish my B.A. because it's wearing me out." Somewhere along the way, through my therapy appointments and quests for resources and support, it had occurred to me that I could be a good therapist because I had empathy for people with misunderstood struggles and I could give them hope. The first order of business, however, was to get myself stronger.

"Yeah, and it looks like you might be self-medicating with a couple things here, so that concerns me," she said, looking at her computer screen.

"Well, it's the stress. I'm getting it from all sides and I have no time for myself," I said, tapping my foot.

"Oh, honey. I know, and you're sensitive; I can see that. Maybe try other coping tools like meditation or walking, or whatever works for you. Alcohol can be highly addictive," she said empathetically, in a tone that reminded me of Karen the nurse and Tricia the social worker. All these women who were warm and generous and made me feel validated and normal. My string of paper suns was with me still.

"OK, I will watch it and also try to cut down on smoking," I said, imagining myself refraining from the compulsion to smoke and drink, and feeling better. "I can do this."

"Yes, and come see me in another year. If you can't stop or slow down, see me sooner so we can talk about getting help. Self-care is important while you're doing so much for everyone else. I want to see you in that equation as well, sweetie. You deserve it. Other people have options besides you to get their needs met."

I was relieved. Not only did she not lecture me, but she was encouraging. On my way out, I made an appointment for the next year. It occurred to me that I couldn't go on indefinitely without taking care of myself. The concept was so strange, but I had seen how my body had changed over time with the stress I was under—the weight gain, high blood pressure, emotional eating and drinking, and fatigue. And didn't I deserve a good life, especially when I was working so hard to give that to others? I realized that my body had never belonged to me. As a child, I was another hand and my uncle's sex object; as a teenager and young adult, I was a mom and caregiver. My body was property of the church and the system. Purity culture that I was raised in didn't acknowledge consent or allow agency. I was even responsible for men wanting me. Self-care and boundaries—even self-respect—were misconstrued as selfishness, and yet my doctor was advocating that I focus on myself. It was also clear that a man would not make me happy, as I had been taught. Only I could.

Chapter 30: Hosting the Devil

It is one of those days I feel like I'm learning to be peaceful in my own skin and my apartment is like a sanctuary. I want to stay in this feeling for as long as I can. Minneapolis is welcoming, especially the alternative crowd. Maybe I can live away from the church and be OK.

Rummaging around in my dresser, not finding many good options to wear, I settle on a beige cotton tank top with white trim and a pair of jean shorts from the Gap. My uncle Harold had called the day before to ask me to get together. It has been years since I have seen him, and I think he might be supportive of my recent exit from the church since he is one of the few from the church who has also left.

Around 1:00 p.m., I finally leave my apartment, shutting both my heavy apartment door and the green wooden slat door. I put my pack of Marlboro Lights in my right pocket, with a lighter inside the pack. My ID and money are in my left pocket.

On the way to my parents' in my red Ford Taurus, I listen to R.E.M., The Cranberries, and Alanis Morissette. When Dolores O'Riordan sings "Dreams," I know I am on my way.

Harold and I have a smoke together when I get to my parents'. He is already standing outside waiting for me and chatting with my brothers.

I flick my cigarette butt onto the gravel driveway and start toward the front door when he stops me. "Hey, did you want to get going?" he asks. I hadn't expected that we would be leaving right away, but I am agreeable. It is 2:00 p.m.

"Are you kids smoking out there?" Mom confronts me at the doorway.

"I just had a cig with Uncle Harold, but the younger kids aren't smoking," I reassure her.

After a brief conversation with my family, I leave.

Uncle Harold rides with me in my car and questions me about my life, so I ask him jokingly if this is an investigation. With a serious tone and a low voice, he says gruffly, "No, but I do know how to get people to cooperate if I need to." Slightly shocked and confused, I keep driving in silence.

Not knowing what else to do, I put on the radio to KQRS, a station that plays music from the 1960s and 70s, because I think they would have music that he would like. On my way to college classes in the mornings, I listen to their morning show to learn how to make conversation and joke with people so my day's interactions go well. The awkward host, Terry, makes me feel less insecure about my innocent, reticent personality and "ditzy" lack of social awareness.

When we get to Minneapolis, he asks me to show him my apartment. "What are these paper suns you have strung along your ceiling?" he queries me.

"It's my happy place," I reveal. "I don't feel so alone when they're around."

"I could really use a cold beer on a hot day like this," he says with an expression that almost seems impulsive, like his manner when he wanted to leave my parents'.

"Oh! There is a place right across the street from me. It's called Liquor Lyle's. I'm underage, though, so I don't know if I could get in now that the bouncers are probably out." He looks at me like he is studying me, and I feel weird.

His face lights up. "Let's check it out! I'll get us in," he states with the confidence of someone who is accustomed to getting his way. As we walk across the street, he grabs my hand and holds it. I don't resist because I am stunned and don't want to be rude.

He orders an endless stream of drinks and insists on sharing them with me. It doesn't feel like I can say no because he paid for them. I also keep drinking because I am scared and don't know why. He holds my hand most of the night and tells me how lucky he is to be out with such a pretty girl. The conversation is a blur.

When we get back to my apartment at 1:00 a.m., I am drunk and exhausted. He takes my hand and whispers into my ear, "I had such a good time with you tonight. You're a special girl. I've been lonely since I lost your Auntie Rose. It wasn't a happy marriage either." He didn't explain why it wasn't happy or admit that he had abandoned her. He also talked about coming back from the Vietnam War and how there wasn't "PTSD" then—they drank beer and partied in downtown Minneapolis and went on with life like it was nothing.

I am too intoxicated to think about what he is saying and I can't form an articulate response, but I sympathize with what I think is his grief. My body freezes, and my mind stops working. And as I lean away from him, I lose my balance and almost fall into my bookshelf. He grabs my arm to steady me and doesn't let go. He strokes my arm and speaks like he is confiding in me, "I've been really depressed, but it feels great to be with you. I think we can relate, since you told me about being lost after leaving the church."

He is eager, and I am disoriented. Then he kisses me lightly on the mouth, and I don't react—like I'm a statue. The whole situation makes no sense to me.

"I've wanted you for a very long time. You were such a darling little girl back in Phoenix. I hope you know that you are the most

beautiful girl in the family." Hardly anyone told me I was pretty because in the church it was vain to focus on looks and to the world I was plain without makeup.

Little by little, he leads me to my bed. My head is spinning, and I want to throw up. Dazed and under his spell, I do what I am told. He tells me to lie down on the bed, which is my comfy spot for reading books and playing with my cats. I can hardly keep my eyes open.

"We're just two people," he tries to convince me. "It doesn't matter if we're related."

I try not to move, hoping that will make him go away—like playing dead if a wild animal is about to attack you. He instructs me to relax and not worry like he is ordering someone he is arresting. He pulls his belt off. It is like being in one of those dreams when you try to run away, but your legs won't move.

Fading out and trying not to think about what is happening, I feel him moving.

"I hope you don't mind that I'm doing this, but you have to admit that it feels really fucking amazing," he says. He sucks and licks my breasts and begins to feel down my shorts. I have no time to react before he is touching me everywhere.

"Oh, yeah, I hope you're good and wet for me," he growls into my ear. Getting up, he unbuttons my shorts and yanks them off. My body bounces limply on my bed. Then my flower-print underwear are off. He pushes my legs apart and jams his finger into my vagina, hard enough that I wince. It's already happening, and I feel powerless to stop him.

"Don't move; stay there," he orders me, not allowing his plan to be interrupted. That's when I feel his warm tongue in between my legs, running up and down my clitoris and poking inside my vagina. I am lifeless.

"I'm going to fuck you, but you don't need to be concerned; I had a vasectomy."

My uncle's warm semen spills out of my vagina as I try not to open my drunken, ashamed eyes that feel like cement. Squinting, I can vaguely see his silhouette, quickly putting on his pants. "Thanks, sweetheart. You're not only a pretty face; you're a good fuck," he says to me, as though I willingly gave him my body.

I hardly remember driving him back to my aunt's house after I sobered up while he talked incessantly like we had just made love. I try to act like nothing ever happened—try to block it out—and make conversation with him as best I can by uttering one-word responses. He is jubilant. I am dead inside. Digging around in my shorts pocket, I find my cigarettes, and light one after the other, as if I can smoke the memories out of my head.

Pulling up the driveway of her house, he forcibly kisses me on the mouth again like we had been lovers. As he walks up the front walk to the house, I clench the steering wheel. Men know that they can get away with fucking me, and that's all I am to them—my sex organs. Even to my own uncle. Maybe the church people are right that I am a slut—maybe I deserve it.

On the long drive home, I feel like a shell of myself—I feel nothing. I smoke cigarettes and look at the radiant moon mostly obscured by ominous clouds and think it must be as lonely as I am.

Chapter 31: Money Is Time

Imani and I moved into the apartment in Wayzata, and I was able to see how our belongings would fill up a home of our own, without being mixed with multiple other people's things or scattered throughout someone else's house. Imani's toddler bed was on one side of the bedroom, and my parents gave me a mattress with a metal frame that I placed on the other side of the room.

I put all of Imani's stuffed animals on the floor, with the biggest in back and the smallest in front. On the walls, I taped up her drawings and artwork, like hand and foot prints we had made together—then my string of paper suns. My green metal bar table and chairs that I had bought with a bad check went under the outdated chandelier near the kitchen. My parents also gave me their old La-Z-Boy recliner that went near the patio door, in view of the clunky television that I still had from my apartment in Uptown. Next to the recliner, I put Imani's high chair, where she could watch television, eat, and do activities like coloring.

On an afternoon, after I finished moving everything, I brought Imani to see our new apartment. I proudly showed her where her bed was, how all of her favorite stuffed animals were there in organized fashion to greet her, and where she could play in our back yard we shared with the other residents. Imani picked up one of her dolls and ran around the whole apartment with incoherent gleeful sounds, and then came back to hug my legs and squeal, "Mama, my house!"

We spent the afternoon playing in our new home. We had a tea party with the stuffed animals and ate ice cream and painted our nails. It was the most fun we had had in a while, until I had to take Imani back to my parents' home so I could go back to Cubby's for my evening shift.

I tried to use the time on the road to teach and entertain Imani—singing, talking, and pointing out interesting sights along the way. Whenever we drove past a Mobil gas station and saw a winged, flying red horse, Pegasus, I said, "There's your horse!" And I said the same thing when we drove past the horse and feed supply store, with a tarnished black horse on a pole. I kept cassette tapes in my car to play stories and songs. Everything I was able to give her made me feel rich. The world was full of riches.

* * *

On one of our routine physical therapy days, we got to Courage Center a few minutes late because I had to coordinate childcare for my siblings and the main parking lot was full. So I had to carry Imani from the overflow lot. I was excited to tell Kelly about our new apartment.

As we walked up to the pediatric entrance, I saw the usual paratransit buses, like Metro Mobility, waiting or dropping people off. They didn't wait very long if riders were late—a few minutes and they left. Some people (a few in wheelchairs and a few standing or sitting) were waiting—often well past their pickup times.

Courage Center had an array of services for people across disabilities, and not all of them were physical or apparent. Some people were autistic, or had brain injuries, or strokes, or spinal cord injuries, or intellectual disabilities, etc.—

sometimes a combination. They also had a lot of sports and recreation programs.

As a nursing student and caregiver, I had learned about some of the many types of disabilities and how complex they are. Getting to know many people in their individual situations taught me even more. I learned about, and gained an appreciation for, the bigger issues surrounding them beyond their disabilities. Communities are inaccessible and not inclusive enough to allow them to fully participate in life; not just wide enough doorways and ramps, but universal spaces and technology designed to provide information for a diverse audience, for example. People are often forced into poverty as a result of the expenses of their disabilities and must stay within income limitations to keep their services and supports, as well as lack of opportunities. Poverty makes everything more challenging and contributes to disability. If you are poor, you are more likely to become disabled, and if you are disabled, you are more likely to become poor. Disability and poverty are deeply connected. We knew that from living it.

Seeing everyone waiting outside, I thought about how much I had waited when I was even poorer than I was now—the long lines at the county, the process of submitting paperwork to overwhelmed government agencies, the gaps between when you needed something and when it was available, which could be months or years… I always felt trapped, lonely, powerless, and without dignity. It reminded me of the oppressive nature of the church.

I said hello to Kesha, who rolled past us in a wheelchair, and waved at Abdi, who was waiting for his ride. There were a lot of us regulars who got to know each other. At the door was a teenage girl with cerebral palsy named Chloe who liked to talk to Imani.

"Hi, sweetie," she said, taking a couple steps closer. Imani giggled and said hi back.

"That's a cute little unicorn you have today." She smiled.

"It's from my birthday!" Imani said happily.

"Ah, cool! Have fun at therapy. It's time for me to go home now. They tired me out today," she said, her sparkling eyes defying her fatigue.

Older people with disabilities reacted like this to Imani—delighted and warm-hearted, like they were looking out for her because they knew more about how the world was when you're disabled and they wanted to pad her with layers of love and affirmation to protect her from the inevitable wear and tear of ableism and discrimination.

Chloe walked away using her forearm crutches, and I thought that the way she walked was part of who she was, like her kindness and interest in comic books. And if there were more people as cool as Chloe, disabled or not, maybe the future could be bright for kids like Imani.

The prospect of Imani having to battle suffocating adversity her whole life simultaneously depressed and galvanized me to rebel against these crushing systems that kept people down. I thought about how I had disentangled myself from the church as best I could and found myself in another web of controlling systems that brought food scarcity, housing instability, long work hours, low wages, little free time, healthcare concerns, transportation issues, childcare costs, legal battles, minimal recourse to deal with problems, and overall, a myriad of socioeconomic barriers that both inhibited my ability to develop and contribute and threatened the survival of my baby and me. Being a caregiver, I had seen firsthand how these systems affected other people, as well. Mark was forced to keep his income low enough to be eligible for Medicaid so he could have basic healthcare and qualify for PCA supports. It was ludicrous!

Now that I knew so much more about the conditions of communities for many of us, I felt a deep sense of responsibility to help fix it. I had not been on the other side of the systems I interacted with, so I had no clue where to begin, but I would make inroads somehow, some way. Of that I was sure. We had big problems, and people were hurting, and it was unacceptable. Certainly, I couldn't be the only one to come to this conclusion.

Back home, I cleaned our apartment to get ready for Imani's birthday party. She was playing with her Barbie dolls in the bathroom sink, which she had filled up to make a "pool." I asked her if she could move for a minute so I could wash the floor under her stool.

"But I'm not in your way," she said.

"We're having your friends over for your party, so I need to clean up our home," I encouraged her.

"But, mommy! We're not having the party in HERE!" she debated.

Laughing, thoroughly charmed by her wit and spunk, I said, "You seem to have some very good verbal and creative skills, my little litigator." And I gave up washing the floor under her plastic, green and yellow step stool. It delighted me that she knew she could speak her truth to me and that I was raising her to be free.

That weekend, seven friends came over to celebrate Imani's birthday. She had helped me decorate the apartment with streamers and balloons and put frosting on the cake. My mom brought my youngest siblings, and her sister brought her kids who were the same age. A few friends from my high school came with their kids. M'Kayla from down the hall came with her mom. A pile of gifts wrapped in bright colors and stuffed into sparkly bags sat on the living room floor. Imani was in her element with her friends around her as she celebrated turning another year older and being a "big girl." For me, it was a grand moment to be able to do a normal childhood ritual. Afterward, I sent thank you notes with our very own address on the envelope.

Chapter 32: Show Me

Today was Cubby's six-week haircut appointment with Irene in a hot spot area we liked to go, which meant we would be having our usual post-haircut lunch out. We hit up our favorite spots, and if we were feeling adventurous, some random new one.

"Cubby, your hair is getting so long that you're starting to look like a girl," I said, pulling his hair into a ponytail with my fingers.

"I would make a cute one." He winked.

"Of course, you would—those eyes, baby," I said, bouncing my shoulders and wiggling my eyebrows.

"Gigi would have a fit!"

"What would I have a fit about?" Gigi called from the dining room.

"Never mind, mother," Cubby replied. "OK, Bridge, let's get me up."

His wheelchair was sitting next to his bed because Gigi had been sitting in it, watching a morning show with him. After she got up, I pulled her back cushion off and tossed it onto the couch.

Like clockwork, I pressed the bed remote to raise Cubby's head and pulled the pillow out from under his legs. I scratched his head, which was something he loved so much his eyes almost rolled back.

"Do you have any new jokes for Irene today?" I asked.

"Should I tell her the one about the Irish, American, and Polish lawyers?" he asked.

Laughing, as much at my memory of the joke as the expression on Cubby's face, I said, "Yeah, she would get a kick out of that. Plus, I think she laughs at all your jokes regardless, so you have a sympathetic audience."

"Very funny," Cubby said sarcastically.

I swung his legs over the bed, pulled his upper body toward me, scooted his butt out, and stood him up to transfer him into his wheelchair—slowly sitting him down. Then I put the leg rests on and pulled his butt back in the chair by hugging him from behind. We went to the front hall bathroom to brush his teeth and then the kitchen for breakfast. He started with drinking his Citrucel in orange juice with a flexible straw (for regularity) and took his pills with water.

Gigi had poured a bowl of cereal, and I added the milk. No matter what was happening in their lives or in the rest of the world, Gigi laid out her son's breakfast exactly so.

I put on Cubby's apron before I fed him and parked him under the table with the chair brakes on.

"So, have you gotten any child support lately from 'Gotta Live Too?'" Cubby asked. He was helping me get a lot of my financial life in order. I had bought a $100,000 life insurance policy, per his recommendation. At some point, I was going to look into wills and trusts to make sure that Imani's money would be protected in case anything happened to me. Receiving a chunk of money would make her ineligible for SSI and Medicaid, which she still had since Tricia helped me set it up at the hospital.

"Nothing. He says that he doesn't want to pay ME the money and that he needs to focus on building his business so it can pay off for Imani later. And, get this, he claims that he wasn't at the court hearing when child support was ordered, even though he was and we have a court order signed by the judge."

"Fuck him," Cubby said, shaking his head. "You know what, Bridge, some of the people in your life have been criminal to you. If I could move my hands, I would strangle them."

Whenever Cubby was indignant like this, I thought, *You know what, he's right.* But the way I was treated was so normal to me that I didn't realize how bad it was until someone else highlighted it.

"So, I wanted you to look at some paperwork I have in my bag for child support, to get your opinion," I said.

"Of course," Cubby said. "The government hasn't done a goddamn thing."

I took the papers out of the big envelope from Supportkids.com—Child Support Enforcement. Their motto was "Because our children deserve a world of support."

I read Cubby what I had in my application so far:

Marcus operates his own business, "Super Fresh Services," and claims to be "big" and have considerable business connections. He has claimed that through his success in this operation, Imani (child) will never have a financial need for anything, including college. He acknowledges that he makes enough money to meet support obligations, however he feels that, "I need to live, too," and putting money into his business would pay off better for her (child) later in her life.

Marcus does not file correctly on his tax returns. He has bragged of his ability to disguise improper figures reported to IRS.

Marcus drives a Dodge Neon, plate #339-YAX, which may or may not belong to a former girlfriend, Tina, with whom he shares second child (Marina, D.O.B. – 06/10/1999).

**Please do not allow Marcus to know where the information I have furnished has come from. (That I was the informant.) – Thanks.*

"Very good," Cubby said. "Very good."

I finished feeding him breakfast, draped his apron over his chair, and rinsed out his dishes in the sink.

Irene was busy with another customer when we arrived at her salon, so we waited next to an elderly woman who was reading a magazine. Cubby asked me to adjust his arms, and I got up to move them back. The woman put her magazine down slightly and said, "You are such a dear to help him."

"You don't know what he puts up with," I joked. "I'm more high maintenance than he is."

Cubby started laughing, and it triggered a spasm, so his whole body clenched up and his legs shook. Needing some levity after talking about child support problems that morning, I started cracking up but tried to stifle it. I got up and stood in front of Cubby while I pushed his legs down to stop the spasms. We looked at each other directly in the eyes and busted up again at our wonderful, smartass relationship and its juxtaposition to the general public's perception of disability and caregiving.

"So, Cubby, what are we doing today, honey?" Irene asked. "Do you want a spike?"

"I'll give you fifty bucks if you do it." I nudged her.

Cubby stuck his tongue out at both of us in the mirror, and we laughed. Irene asked Cubby about his kids and me about Imani. She told Cubby that her husband had bought a pontoon and that he should come out on the lake with them. The lake culture was in full swing. It wasn't safe to transfer him onto a boat, but it was nice to think about. Cubby was waiting for a cure so he could do things like that again.

"Bridge, can you give Irene the check in my wallet that Gigi filled out?" Cubby asked. I pulled his wallet out of his backpack that hung on the back of his wheelchair. It was where we kept all the important things like money, pills, paperwork, and the urinal.

We scheduled Cubby's next appointment at the front of the salon and went down the street to a popular restaurant right on the lake. A lot of people were out—mainly moms with children in strollers and businesspeople.

We were lucky to get a table outside in the back overlooking the lake, considering it was such a good weather day and busy.

Every few minutes, I held up Cubby's iced tea to see if he wanted a sip, unless he told me himself, saying, "Drink me." A woman with a yappy dog sat down next to him, and the dog ran around under his wheelchair and between the tires.

In a hoarse attempt to raise his voice, Cubby said, "Get your fucking dog out of here!"

The woman didn't hear him and kept talking loudly with her friend.

"Bridge, tell that bitch to get her dog out of my sight," Cubby said angrily.

I nervously tapped the woman on the shoulder, "Ma'am, would you mind moving your dog to the other side of the table? It's bothering my friend here." The woman said nothing and turned to her friend and rolled her eyes. They said something I couldn't hear to each other and chuckled.

"That bitch," Cubby said. "No class at all."

Our waiter brought our food: Cubby's fish and chips and my grilled chicken sandwich. "Can I get you anything else?" he asked.

Not being accustomed to speaking up for myself or for anyone else, I hesitated, but then realized that I had to fix the issue of the dog. My body tensed up, almost like an internal version of one of Cubby's spasms. "Yeah, can you see if they can have the dog sit on the other side of the table so it isn't bothering my friend here?"

The waiter asked the woman to move her dog, and she was very amenable to him but snorted at Cubby and me after he left.

And yet, she moved her dog! I was a bit shocked that what I had done had changed someone's behavior. It got me thinking that I could have personal power by standing up to people. Suddenly, I felt taller. Maybe I could even do that for myself.

On October 31, 2000, I received a letter from Supportkids.com – Child Support Enforcement:

Congratulations on taking your first step toward putting Supportkids.com to work for your family. We have your application in hand, and after careful review of all your information, we believe we can help you. You're off to a great start!

We are ready now to notify the government that we will be acting as your representative, and that we have your authorization to deal with them on your behalf.

On February 9, 2001, I received another letter from Supportkids.com:

Dear Bridget Siljander, *Case Number: 232667*

We wanted to confirm with a letter the actions we are taking to close your case with our office.

As you know, Child Support Enforcement, Supportkids.com, has the capacity to affect credit, place liens on non-exempt property and take money from wages. We regret that none of these remedies in addition to the child support enforcement techniques we ordinarily utilize resulted in payment.

We wish you the best of luck in your continued efforts.

Sincerely,

Supportkids.com

Cubby had some choice words for this and promised to help me find a way to squeeze money out of Marcus. "If I have to get up out of this wheelchair and shake him upside down by his feet until the coins fall out."

Chapter 33: Santa Is Female

Arriving at North Hennepin Community College, I put on my backpack and set the diaper bag in the front seat of the car—then opened the back door to reach in to unbuckle Imani, who was still sleeping. Once I had her in my arms, I grabbed the diaper bag and swung it over my shoulder, and then my purse. The air was bitter cold, and I shivered as I rushed my precious, heavy load to the Science building so I wouldn't be late for my 8:00 a.m. precalculus class. My shoes were filled with snow when I arrived, and my feet were turning numb. Miraculously, Imani continued to sleep, but I was ready with food and toys for her the minute she woke up. Since I didn't have much money for childcare, there wasn't much choice in the matter.

I had started college when I was fifteen years old and completed three years of college through the Post-Secondary Enrollment Options (PSEO) program. Then I had attended a registered nursing program until I was too exhausted from the additional full-time job, church stress, and delaying my abortion to reconcile the guilt placed on me for my pregnancy. Fortunately, my two-year associate's degree would transfer as a package to a four-year college or university. I needed to complete the rest of the requirements for a pre-med neuroscience degree. By going to North Hennepin Community College to do as much coursework as I could, it would be more affordable and logistically easier. Tuition was cheaper, and the campus was small and had its own free parking lot.

My arms were burning from carrying Imani and all of our things, and I gladly unloaded her and everything in the back corner of the classroom.

I made a makeshift bed for her on the floor with blankets and covered her up. Her cherub-like face peeked out with rosy cheeks, a tiny nose, and puckered lips. To make a young child attempt to sleep on a thinly carpeted cement floor surrounded by strangers felt like an injustice. This was not what I wanted for my child. While she should have been in a safe, loving, and stimulating environment, she was sitting in the corner of a classroom or car seat in my car during long transports, or languishing elsewhere. Rarely did she have the stability of staying in one place to play with other children her age and be exposed to age-appropriate education. An hour in class with me wasn't the problem—but everything added up to a lot of time spent in dull situations during the most impressionable years of child development. I worried that our poverty would deny her what she needed to grow in all the important ways to succeed in life. All I could do was take all the steps to build a rich life as we went along with the resources available and hope for the best. Still, it outraged me that I was set up by society to struggle.

A tall, blonde girl, who looked like a model, sat in front of me. I had seen her get out of her Mercury Sable car in the parking lot, carrying her notebook. A former pro hockey player who was pre-med turned around in his chair a few times to look at her, and his gaze indicated that he was unaware that I was also in his line of sight.

Imani stirred a little, and I pushed the blankets around her face to shield her from the bright fluorescent lights. I looked at the beautiful blonde hair of the girl in front of me and thought to myself that she must have washed it that morning because it looked fresh and dry. Mine was greasy and in a bun with a clip holding my bangs down. She smelled good—like flowers and vanilla, and leisure. Cupping my hand, I exhaled a few breaths into my hand to see if I had bad breath since I couldn't remember if I had time to brush my teeth that morning. As the rest of the class took their seats, I looked at them self-consciously to observe if they noticed me—and my domestic situation in the corner. I leaned forward to try to hide Imani from their sight. Nobody seemed to care as they sat down. One boy yawned into the sleeve of his skater hoodie and slouched further down in his chair. Another girl rolled her eyes at someone she sat next to that she must have known, like she was annoyed to be there.

Mr. Hough, the instructor, had not given me permission to bring Imani to class, and I hadn't asked—there was an unspoken agreement that it was acceptable as long as it was not addressed. Mr. Hough lectured by doing problems on the white board. It all seemed to make sense during class, but homework was a different story. What he wrote and the problems I saw in the textbook just didn't align.

* * *

At 9:00 a.m., I carried Imani and our things back to the car to go back to Cubby's so he could get up for the day. We were living with him and Gigi for a couple months while Gigi recovered from a mastectomy. It was freezing in the car, and the heat blew cold for the first few minutes before it gradually warmed up. "Look, Imani, you can see your breath!" I puffed toward her. "Mommy is making a cloud!" She giggled and opened her mouth, but no vapor came out. "You have to blow like this, baby: huh, huh!" She opened her mouth again and tried to imitate me, but nothing happened. We both laughed together, and she scrunched up her eyes like she did when she was excited. "You were a good girl at mommy's school," I praised her, followed by kissing sounds.

"Yah," she said, kicking her legs, and put a Cheerio in her mouth.

* * *

Back at Cubby's, I unloaded Imani from the car and gathered all of our things again, plus my backpack. He needed help, and Imani was antsy. I plunked Imani in front of one of the televisions and tended to Cubby.

If I could graduate from college and make a better life for her, with minimal scrapes along the way, she could be given a much more interesting and meaningful future. I knew that nobody was going to give it to us and that we had to fight for it—rather, I had to fight for it for the both of us. But she would have to fight alongside me. My mind was made up. I wasn't going to lie down and take it anymore! The gloves were off.

* * *

Later that evening, I took Imani to see the Harry Potter holiday show in downtown Minneapolis on the top floor of a department store. I had been reading the series to her. It was inspiring that J. K. Rowling, a former struggling single mom, who had an unhappy childhood and dealt with depression, adversity, and poverty, had written the books. I imagined one day looking back on these years and feeling accomplished—and giving back. My story was not over yet.

"Imani, do you want Harry Potter glasses for Christmas?" I asked.

"I want a magic wand!" she requested.

Chapter 34: Love Is an Artist

The air was fresh and chilly in the posh downtown area near my apartment, with a light breeze coming off the lake. I thought I would energize and warm up at a café with a small black coffee, which I could barely afford, while I waited. Feeling nervous, I fidgeted at a table outside, adjusting my sunglasses. My neighbor Doug had asked me to meet his friend Charles, whose father needed a caregiver.

Then, out of the corner of my eye, walking toward me along the sidewalk past the Ben & Jerry's, I spotted a well-dressed, balding, dark-haired man wearing bifocals. Squinting as he lowered his head, he asked, "Are you Bridget?"

For a few minutes, while I sipped my coffee, Charles told me about his parents. Clearly, he was close to them, but I wasn't sure what I could help them with, except to offer some ideas.

We kept talking, long after our coffees were finished, and took a stroll down the railroad track near the lake.

* * *

The next day, Charles called me to tell me what a great time he had meeting me and how much he enjoyed our conversation.

"Thanks," I said. "I had a nice time, too, but you are too old for me to date. But I would like to be friends." I wasn't sure what to make of our meeting, but it actually did feel like a date.

* * *

For the next weeks and months, Charles called me at least daily. He began coming over to visit me and Imani and keep us company, even if he just sat in the recliner while I tended to Imani's needs. The three of us visited the Minnesota Zoo, went out to dinner, and watched movies together. Imani often convinced "Cha-wohls" to play with her, and he taught her how to paint. Charles became the first person I called when I had stress or dilemmas. He was always happy to help. It was almost biblical: "For I was hungry and you gave me something to eat, I was thirsty and you gave me something to drink, I was a stranger and you invited me in, I was sick and you looked after me, I was in prison and you came to visit me." I believed that Charles would never betray me, and I had faith in him.

* * *

On a late winter morning, I woke up with Imani curled up next to me in her onesie pajamas. Her hair was sticky from playing with her food the day before. I looked at her face, which somehow still looked animated when she was sleeping, with her pouty lips that Jessica always loved. Her fat little hands that loved to make art and play with dolls, her round, well-fed belly, and wispy blonde hair made up a happy, wonderful girl. While she slept, I had a moment to reflect on how much I loved her before she would be up and buzzing with energy once again and demanding my attention. Her leg braces with a Tweety Bird print were lying on the floor next to the bed. Every morning, before she bounded out of bed, we did her leg stretches and put her braces on. It was a normal part of the day, like putting on her clothes and shoes.

"Good morning, princess," I said quietly as I stroked her cheek. Her eyelids fluttered, and she turned over, away from me. Rubbing her back, I sang her "Mary Had a Little Lamb." She had a small plastic sheep that she named "Mary" and inspired by the song, she took it everywhere she went.

Still facing away from me, she said, "Mom, I like Mary. She's my little lamb."

"And you're my little lamb," I said.

We snuggled for a few more minutes, and then she was impatient to get going for the day. She squirmed off the bed and had a pretend conversation with a pretend person with her toy phone.

"Hi, I'm going to school to-DAY. I can make a pic-chow fo YOU!"

"Come here, Imani, we need to do your stretches, honey," I coaxed her.

"I'm talking to my friend, Emma-wee, Mommy."

"Just for a little bit, OK? Then you can put on your birdie braces."

"I don't need them, I can walk already," she insisted.

She didn't like to wear shoes, either.

* * *

That afternoon, after I worked at Cubby's, we went to her three-times-a-week physical therapy appointment. Kelly worked on exercises with Imani and gave us new printouts of Imani's home program: go up and down stairs holding a railing; go up and down a step stool holding my hands; stretch calves by flexing foot up and down; stretch hamstrings with straight leg raises. Today, Imani walked the hallways using her walker. Kelly and I pretended to run away from her and she chased us.

I asked Kelly if Imani would ever walk steadily without her walker because her first physical therapist said that she never would. "Her hips are too tight," the therapist had said.

Kelly replied, "Well, she is still very young and she mainly needs it for gait training and distance now. We will keep working, and she's making really strong progress." I tried to find current information on long-term outcomes for CP, but there wasn't much out there. Nobody had clear answers. All I ever heard was that the part of the brain that caused it was "static," or unchanging. Thus, I assumed the focus was on rehabilitating the neuromuscular effects, which would either stay the same or improve.

Next up was occupational therapy. Rita gave Imani two pieces of paper with pattern templates printed on them and a pair of scissors. One had the parts of a paper doll: head, shirt, skirt, arms, and legs. The other had the parts of a snowman: three circles for the body, arms, and plastic eyes.

She explained the process. "Imani, you're going to cut around the black lines to cut out the parts." Then she demonstrated by cutting out one of the snowman circles. "See?"

Imani giggled. "I'm gonna make a snowman today with YOU!" She pointed a finger at Rita.

Her effervescent personality melted hearts. Rita mouthed to me, "She is adorable!"

Rita gave Imani verbal encouragement as she worked hard to cut out the shapes, then helped her glue them onto empty toilet paper rolls.

I was so pleased that Imani was treated like any other child her age and that her supports and services didn't feel clinical. She had fun and wanted to do the activities that Rita, Kelly, and others introduced her to. Watching Imani learn was so rewarding—much like the gardening that I did back home when I poured seeds into the soil and tended the plants until glorious flowers sprang from them. It made my heart sing to see her eyes twinkle with understanding after straining to comprehend, and her jubilant smile when she accomplished something that she struggled with. Part of her "homework" was to work on buttoning her shirts and holding scissors, pencils, and crayons. We did lots of crafts at home, finding ideas online now that we had a computer.

Since she was in my belly, I had made sure that art was a part of her life. Art reminds us that what is different is beautiful, what is absurd is fascinating, and what is strange is original. Perhaps through art we could finally learn to appreciate each other.

When we moved to our apartment, I had ordered a subscription for Shirley Temple videos from a commercial I had seen on Cubby and Gigi's television. Now that we had our own place again, and had moved out of my parents', we could watch television—something that was still forbidden by The Controlling Codependent Church, as it should have been named. Shirley Temple reminded me of Imani because she was precocious and had the same darling face and clever eyes.

I popped the VHS tape into our VCR and started *Bright Eyes*—a movie about an orphaned girl who goes to live with a rich family. In a way, we were like two orphan girls ourselves.

Since Imani and I had watched this movie so many times, we sang along to the songs, like "Good Ship Lollipop." After making us some dinner, I put her in her high chair in front of the TV and sat in the recliner.

"Do you want to wear your hair like Shirley Temple?" I asked her. When I grew up in the church, we couldn't color our hair, but we could curl it or put it in rollers. I had bought pink sponge foam rollers that you put in when your hair is damp at bedtime. Waking up in the morning, you'd pull them out and you have ringlets that you can pull apart and style.

"Yeah! And you do it, too!" she said. "Both of us!"

* * *

That night when I came back from working at Cubby's, Imani was asleep. Charles had been babysitting Imani and was waiting up for me, sitting in the recliner, and I told him to wait a minute. I went into my closet and rummaged around, pulling a small, boxy suitcase down from the top shelf. Inside, I kept a bottle of vodka and a small glass. Discreetly, I unscrewed the top and poured myself a large shot that I downed in one gulp. I shivered as it burned my mouth and down my throat. Then I changed into a mini skirt and a shimmery white top (sans bra) and looked in my bathroom mirror to make sure that my cleavage was perky and my hair sexy.

Before going back into the living room, I took another small shot. It could have been a placebo effect, but my body warmed and relaxed and I felt ready. Charles had shown me that he was capable of being my rock and someone who would have my back. He wasn't like the other guys who thought I was easy because I already had a kid. Over the course of hours of conversations, he knew almost everything about me and yet he was not deterred.

"Hey there," I said, as I stood in the hallway at the entrance to the living room and tilted my hips.

Charles looked taken aback.

"Can you close the blinds?" I asked him, the shadows of the streetlights accentuating all of my curves.

Without saying anything, he put the footrest down on the recliner and obliged me. When he turned around, I was walking toward him.

Charles laughed nervously. "Are you feeling OK? To what do I owe this surprise?"

"Well," I said slowly, "I think you are wonderful, and you are making me fall in love with you."

"Then I'm a lucky man. But you know that I'm not trying to sleep with you. I genuinely care about you and Imani. I would be here if we never got intimate."

"I know, and that's why I feel comfortable with you, and why I waited to do this," I stated my case. "You can sit down," I told him as I walked to the recliner and sat on the armrest.

I pulled up my skirt a little. The safety I felt with him was an aphrodisiac.

"I want you to go down on me," I said as I lay down on the floor. He got up, still fully clothed, and kneeled down between my legs. He looked at me hesitantly as if to ask if I was sure, and I responded by looking at him intently to urge him to get started already.

As I started to orgasm, the room seemed to turn upside down and I became nauseous. Everything became distorted like a carnival house.

"Stop, stop! I feel sick. I'm sorry. You have to go home," I plead, gasping for breath. I couldn't move; I lay paralyzed on the floor as the room spun around me.

Charles' face looked like Uncle Harold's, and a fusion of both of their faces seemed to dance around in front of me like a hellish vision. They had similar hair—dark, balding, and combed the same way. Uncle Harold had been fifty when he raped me, and Charles was currently in his mid-forties. I saw Uncle Harold on top of me again like I was eighteen—telling me that we were *"just two people."*

"You're such a pretty girl. I've always thought you were so pretty, since you were little. Make me happy and let me touch you, sweetheart." I wanted to tear my own brain out of my terrorized head.

* * *

The next morning, still reeling from the night before and feeling ashamed, I called Charles to explain what had happened.

"I am so sorry if there is anything I could have done differently," he told me, with heavy remorse in his voice. "I would never want to hurt you in any way or be the cause of distress."

Charles was furious with Uncle Harold and told me that what he had done was a heinous crime and he should be in prison. A month later, Imani and I moved in to Charles' house, where we would be safe.

Chapter 35: Education Takes a Village

For the first day of school, I had set my alarm and Imani's Hello Kitty clock (with a nightlight) to get us up early. My alarm went off first, and Imani was still fast asleep, nestled in her bed with her stuffed animals and dolls. Quietly, I crawled in her bed, between her and the bed rail. For a few minutes, I rested with her.

All we had been through flooded my mind: when I was pregnant and promised my baby that she would have a great life; the first moment I saw her in the incubator and cried because she was so beautiful; washing her baby clothes in the Minneapolis apartment building; taking her to the beach for the first time in her car seat; getting her tricycle adapted for her physical therapy; surprising her with a cat who surprised us with kittens; calling her nicknames, like "Maners" and "Cricket"; taking her to college classes with me; all of the times we had moved; trips to the food shelf and human services offices; going to doctor appointments; hauling back and forth to work; and all of the drama we'd been through with Marcus.

This was one of those moments I had dreamed of: my healthy, happy little girl taking flight. She was full of life and bright and had many advantages now.

As for me, I was still a misfit. It had been a relief when the kindergarten open house was over one evening the week before and we could go home. All the other families went to their nice cars while I tried to sneak away with Imani to our old faded baby-blue Topaz at the far end of the parking lot. I would have to take my nose ring out. The other (older) suburban moms would never approve. They appeared to have cookie-cutter lives, and I was a subdued punk with a cynicism for convention.

"Cheeky wants to go to school now," I said as I danced Cheeky on her arms. She giggled and grabbed her little friend. That made me laugh. Cheeky was a Kacheek Neopet—a short, blue, shy character who likes to make new friends (according to a description in his packaging).

Then Imani yawned and smiled at the same time. Fresh from her bath the night before, I helped her get dressed in capri pants, a shirt with a butterfly on it, and a light-blue sweatshirt that she had kept from a modeling job. Charles had connected her with his agent, and I wanted her to feel beautiful as a disabled girl. I fixed her hair with two braids, with ribbons at the ends. Her backpack was already packed with crayons, colored pencils, erasers, #2 pencils, and notebooks.

As we chattered about school, I had a growing anxiety about what the reality of it would be like for her. *Will she be able to get on and off the bus safely? Will she have someone to sit with? Will the other kids at school be friendly to her? Will they make fun of her disability or ask prying questions about her leg brace and how she walks? What if nobody plays with her at recess? I remember what that was like. Will she be safe on the playground equipment? Will she be able to handle her lunch tray by herself? What if she misses me? Will she be able to find her way?* Along with her registration and enrollment documents, I had sent the school information on the custody agreement—and told them that Marcus was not allowed to take Imani. Although he had stayed away from preschool for the past few years, I couldn't predict what he would do now.

Imani's teacher, a young newlywed with a crew cut and a round face with big brown eyes, relieved some of my worries, including those about how Imani would be treated, when he talked at the open house about appropriate behavior, kindness, and expectations. Already, Imani had made a friend. And yet, I had to see how it would go before I could be calm.

At the bus stop, I took pictures of Imani and her neighborhood friends, who were all giddy for the first day of school. They gave each other bunny ears. Cheeky was in the picture, too.

As the bus left the stop, Imani turned around and waved to me through the window, and I blew her a kiss. My heart ached as the bus drove away with my most precious treasure and disappeared around the corner. She felt so far from me, but I knew it was the best thing for her—and for me.

Since she was born, I had kept her under close watch. She had been surrounded by people I knew well and trusted. At school, there would be many people I didn't know and there was so much uncertainty. But I knew it wasn't the world that the church warned us about; unbelievers were just as nice, or mean, as they were. I taught her about good touch and bad touch so she would know if someone tried to abuse her. I would fucking kill anyone who even thought about it, I vowed.

"You gonna be all right?" Johnny asked me in his southern drawl. His daughter, Sara, was in Imani's grade and they played together.

"Yeah, it's just hard on the first day," I replied, hoping I was right.

"Well, I'll tell you what. I have two grown kids and I bawled when the first one went to school. Then it got to the point that I was glad to get them out of my hair—and now I have no hair left." He chuckled.

Half-crying and half-laughing, I wiped my eyes and said, "My parents probably thought that sometimes with me."

"She'll be fine. Don't you worry," he reassured me.

Feeling a mix of relief, angst, and joy, I nodded my head.

"I'll see you tomorrow," Johnny said.

It was hard to be the only parent for all of these occasions, as well as the day-to-day parenting. I still felt like my nineteen-year-old self who sat desperate at the hospital window and watched all the couples having that experience together. But I was grateful for the encouragement and validation that came from other parents. I looked forward to seeing Johnny in the mornings with his straight talk and sense of humor.

Chapter 36: Hurrah

I was helping Imani do worksheets for school when my cell phone rang. It was my friend Alison. We met when she cheated off of me during English tests in high school. It was then that I became slightly popular via her approval and started getting a sneak peek into what kids who weren't in the church did outside of school. Alison told me about having sex with boys and drinking her mom's booze. Her mom drank a lot and lived with her boyfriend in the trailer park near the high school.

"Hey girlie!" Alison said. "Me and Joanna and Melanie are planning a girls' trip in June, and you should come."

Alison had a daughter two years older than Imani, Joanna had a son two years older, and Melanie had a daughter one year older. All of us had been teen moms.

Every time Alison invited me to something, I felt like that shy, nerdy girl who was being noticed for the first time, and every time I suddenly saw myself as potentially cool. *What the hell,* I thought. I needed to get away from the suburbs and live on the wild side for a couple days—and just be twenty-five. My fleeting youth had not been carefree, so I figured I might as well squeeze a few drops from it before I couldn't.

"Yes, oh my God, girl!" I shrieked. "I totally need to get out. You have no idea!" Charles would be fine with watching Imani, and I could also check with either grandma.

I heard her take a drag off her cigarette with a pop and a puff as she went on, "Rock on, babe. We're going to go to Valleyfair on the first Saturday and then get a hotel at

Treasure Island Resort and Casino. Bring your suit so we can hit the hot tub." She took another drag off her smoke.

We were going to let loose, and I couldn't wait! Alison said that she was bringing her beer bong and I should get a bottle of vodka and Diet Mountain Dew and extra smokes.

One phone call and I had ditched my desire to fit in with those old, stale, vanilla women. As soon as I got off the phone, I ran upstairs to find my duffel bag and start stuffing it with my swim suit and cutest clothes that I would never wear around the school moms. My camera, an extra roll of film, my curling iron, and the sexy underwear that were probably musty—it all went in.

"Agh!" I said to myself. Internally, my young self was rattling the cage. After halfway packing the bag, I ran back downstairs and took a shot of vodka.

I took a cigarette and my lighter and went out to the backyard through the garage. It was early evening, and the sun was beginning to set in the spring sky. Finally, it was sweatshirt weather. The warmth of the vodka settled into my blood, and each inhale of my cigarette was meditative. We were going to have such a blast. These girls knew how to have fun, and I was overdue.

* * *

Life was busy with college and Cubby and, of course, being a mom. I finished another semester, and my grades were good. The countdown had begun. Before I knew it, the girls' weekend had come.

Alison came over on a sunny Saturday morning on her way from the rural town where she lived. Her bleached blonde hair was in a scrunchie and she had on full makeup.

Melanie and Joanna were in the back seat and they rolled down their windows to cheer, "Woohoo! Let's get this party started!" I was hoping that Hildegard, the judgmental housewife next door, wasn't out because otherwise she would look at me funny and make me feel self-conscious forever.

"Do you guys remember when we used to pass notes in class? I just thought of that when you were on your way over."

"Hey, sugar pie, honey bunches of oats, with sugar on top—how could I forget?" Alison said, using one of our salutations. "And Bridget *looked* like the goody-goody religious girl."

"Alison, nobody believes you," I said, and we all laughed. "Besides, you were the one who corrupted me by giving me a makeover in the bathroom during study hall."

"I almost didn't recognize you!" Melanie exclaimed, still looking shocked. "I never saw you with makeup on before!"

"I didn't know you then, Bridge," Joanna said. "But you are a cool chick now. I think Alison turned you loose."

"Yeah, she sure did," I said, puckering my lips and raising one shoulder. "Some of us religious girls rebel the hardest."

We piled into my convertible with the top down and pulled out of the driveway like giddy high school girls. Joanna turned on the radio to a pop station and the Britney Spears song "Toxic" came on. Melanie started to sing along, and we joined her.

At Valleyfair, an amusement park, we parked away from the other cars so we could load up on booze from the trunk. "Which one of you bitches wants a shot?" I asked as I unscrewed the top off the vodka bottle. "Get your lush asses over here before I drink it all."

A truck of shirtless guys drove past us and whistled. "Come and get it!" Joanna hollered, raising a beer. She looked like every young, hot-blooded man's dream: tall, thin—like a supermodel—blonde, and not conspicuously smart enough to intimidate them.

"None of you babes better get pregnant on this trip," Melanie joked. "Oh, that's right, we're all practically married… except Ali."

Alison was too busy slamming her second beer to argue.

"We all have to forget something," she said, wiping her chin. "After a couple of these, I'll have DRS—don't remember shit."

"What the hell do you have to forget?" I asked. "You have the most perfect life of all of us."

"Remember Jason?" she quizzed me. "Jeremy thinks I cheated on him with Jason, and I did—and I can't hide it. I'm like a whore in church when he asks me about Jason. Give me another beer."

"Fuck," I sympathized. "I'm sorry, girl." Not knowing what else to do or say, I handed her another beer and poured myself a big shot of vodka. Then I cracked a can of Diet Mountain Dew and did said shot.

"Woooo!" I burst out and shook my head. "The first one always burns." Two more shots and I was ready to hit the amusement park.

Sufficiently liquored up, we hid a couple beers and a small bottle of vodka on ourselves and locked up the car. At the entrance, we posed for a group photo that we could pick up on our way out. I was sure we looked as drunk as we were.

Waiting in line, we couldn't stop laughing and falling all over each other. "We're going to get kicked out," Alison laughed, slurring her words. "Shut up, Ali," Joanna said, putting her hand over her mouth and almost toppling both of them.

A couple of moms with their kids looked at us like we were a bunch of delinquents. Little did they know, we were their ilk. Today we had a free pass. If someone gave them a babysitter and a couple shots, they could have been us.

Being slightly inebriated, I saw these moms, and my life, from another perspective. I wondered if I was as uptight as they looked to me now—as conventional and withdrawn as I felt I was becoming in the suburbs. Maybe the shift I was trying to fast track was one I should have been fighting. Now I wasn't sure I wanted assimilation. It seemed sad to me—like death. And here I was with my friends, momentarily escaping its inevitability. The church life was like a distant reality to me now as I stood here in my new life, such as it was.

Back at the car, we all took one more round, and I put the top back down. Next stop, Treasure Island Resort and Casino, an hour and fifteen minutes away via a lot of back roads.

Peeling onto the road after a quick pit stop at a gas station, we noticed a truck full of twenty-something guys drive past us. "Speed up!" Alison shouted. I hammered down on the gas and caught up to them, so we were racing down the road.

"I'm going to let them go ahead!" I yelled above the wind.

"Wait!" Alison yelled back. I punched the gas once more and we were neck-and-neck with them.

"Show us your tits!" the guys hollered. One of them mooned us with his very white ass.

Not to be outdone, Alison lifted her shirt and bra to flash these guys. They cheered, "Yeah!"

Melanie turned around and mooned them while kneeling on the back seat and holding onto Joanna.

This escalated their cheering and yelling, which blended together and was getting drowned out by the wind and sound of their loud truck. I slowed down in the right lane and let them fly by.

It was a relief to arrive at Treasure Island Resort and Casino and see that we still had quite a bit of booze left for the night. We settled into our room and changed into our swimsuits.

Alison pulled out her beer bong and set it up in the shower. She assembled it with a large funnel and a long, thick plastic tube. You poured the beer into the funnel and drank it from the other end of the attached tube. Since she was the professional, we watched Alison demonstrate first. She got almost the whole beer down and lost it at the end, spilling a swig of it in the shower.

"Ladies, this is why we do this in the bathroom!" she announced. I tried it next and wasted half the can of beer. A big splash landed on my shirt.

"I'm sticking with vodka," I said, pouring a shot. We were staying put for the night, and I didn't have to worry about driving.

Eventually, we made our way down to the main floor to have dinner. While waiting at the hostess station, a group of guys walked past us to stake their claim at the bar. "Well, how do you rate?" I asked. My smartass comment was an icebreaker—thanks to liquid courage. They told us they were staying for the weekend and had a large boat docked at the marina on the Mississippi River.

After dinner, for the rest of the night, we drank with them on their boat and on the dock. It seemed like a good idea to jump in the water with an unknown blood alcohol level. There were currents in the river that kept pulling us out, so we were constantly swimming back. I wasn't paying attention and suddenly realized that I was getting really far out.

Joanna called out to me, "Bridge! Come closer in!" One of the guys threw me a life jacket, and I swam up to it and grabbed onto it, paddling my feet as hard as I could. But I was moving only slightly compared to the effort. A wind came by and pushed me a little further out.

"Bridge, you have to get back here or the river will carry you out!" Alison yelled, sounding worried. It must have been serious if she was using that tone. She usually threw caution to the wind. Panicking a little, I paddled my feet vigorously to propel myself toward the dock, working against a current.

"Jesus Christ!" Alison burst. "You had me so scared for a minute!"

The guys helped me up onto the dock and I sat trying to catch my breath. "Someone give me a damn shot," I said.

We stayed for another hour with the guys and decided to go back to our room for girl time. My adventure on the river shook me up. *What the fuck was I doing when I have a girl back home who needs me?* I thought.

For the rest of the night, we drank a little and enjoyed girl talk. Perhaps to prove to ourselves that we still had it, we took topless photos on my camera and laughed about who would have to see them when they were developed.

* * *

Going home the next day in the early afternoon, we were hung over and ready to return back to normal life, but I felt weirdly anxious. Even Hildegard was almost a welcome distraction.

Chapter 37: Worlds Colliding

School was going better than expected for Imani, but I wanted to continually make sure she was included. There was a lot of pressure to keep up with all the other families, and there was an unspoken competition amongst the parents. People seemed nice, but there was a culture of being hyper critical and judgmental. In the hallways at school when I dropped Imani off, I heard snippets of conversations between parents.

"Darling girls—their parents must spend a fortune on their clothes."

"Did you hear that Simon is already in the gifted program? His parents think he's a genius."

"The Johnsons are transferring their kids to a private school where they start Chinese in first grade."

"That mom doesn't volunteer at the school, so who knows what she does all day."

Each morning, I dressed Imani in a cute outfit and did her hair. Each afternoon, I met her at the bus stop to walk her home and give her a snack. She went to Home Base, a childcare program at the school, for the second half of the day. The University of Minnesota gave me childcare assistance to help pay for it. It was part of the Student Parent Help Center, which also had a support group that I never had time to go to. Charles was helpful at times, and I needed him, but our relationship was strained, and it was stressful living in his house with his rules—much like being at my parents' place. He kept his house extremely clean and wanted it very tranquil, so I referred to it as a museum, and he was irritable when Imani's friends came over for playdates. His mood was often dark and despairing.

I helped Imani with schoolwork and projects and crafts for the holidays. I read to her every night until she wanted her back tickled as she fell asleep holding Cheeky, surrounded by her favorite toys and stuffed animals. After a long day at school, and sometimes Cubby's, I occasionally zonked out, briefly, and dragged myself to the computer to do homework. Cubby and Gigi called me a lot to fill in, and I always said yes—leaving even less time for my full academic load.

Being on the University of Minnesota campus was empowering, even with my workload and increasingly common hangovers. Walking along University Avenue, I admired the architecture of the old buildings, juxtaposed by modern amenities. Sharing the same space as kids right out of high school and older students and people from every background was a kind of equalizer. My identity was a college student there, and it didn't matter where I had come from—only where I was going. And I felt that I had my chance to go places here. Imani's mom was going to make something of herself and not let her down. Being with people my own age was also a respite from the older moms I floundered around with.

One night, similar to many other nights, Imani and I went upstairs to her room to put some of her Halloween costume together: black leggings, a black sweater, a do-it-yourself microphone—and my old purple club wig.

I ran the bath water and put in her bubble bath from her Bugs Bunny bottle and dumped in her toys, which were kept in a mesh bag that hung on the shower wall with suction cups. There were foam letters of the alphabet, rubber duckies,

Barbies, an octopus, a wind-up boat, and bath crayons that she could use to draw on the bathtub and shower.

The water ran in the tub, and I ran downstairs to take a shot of vodka, chased by Diet Mountain Dew. It would be a couple hours before I would be able to go to bed, so I took one more shot for good measure. When I got back upstairs, the tub was still filling and Imani was playing with her Polly Pockets—tiny plastic dolls that resembled Barbies with rubber clothes. Now I trusted that I would be relaxed and focused until Imani was asleep. I sat down on the floor to play with her. I was not only her mom, but also her primary playmate.

Tonight I was writing a paper that was due the next day, and I still had to finish the readings. Clearly, there was not enough time to read anything thoroughly, so I skimmed, highlighting anything I thought was relevant. It was another long night, and it took more vodka to get through it.

* * *

The next morning, I drove Imani to school so she could sleep in a little later. As we walked in the front doors, we heard the bell ring, meaning that she was late. We went to the front office to check in. I hated having to go into the school feeling and looking like a wreck, but it was all in the name of making life a teensy-weensy bit easier for Imani. My face was puffy, and I hadn't even put on a bra or brushed my teeth yet.

"I'm sorry that I'm dropping her off late; this is Imani Vega," I apologized to the secretary—a middle-aged woman with short brown hair and black oval glasses. Just then, the principal walked by and overheard me saying Imani's name. *Oh, great,* I thought. *This is going to be the principal's first impression of me: a trashy mom who doesn't have her shit together.* But he looked past me.

"Are you Imani Vega?" he asked her, crouching down to get at eye level. He was about fifty with salt and pepper hair and he wore a pink bow tie.

Imani nodded.

"Great, because I need to meet with you and your mom to talk about a 504 Plan," he said.

He then explained to me that a 504 Plan was something related to special education and we needed to look at it because of her disability status. We would need to have a meeting with Imani's "team"—teachers and staff at the school involved with her education—to discuss any needed accommodations.

"We want to level the playing field for her," he continued. "It's not special treatment; it's about equality and fairness and it's based on a civil rights law called the Rehabilitation Act. There is also a federal law called the Americans with Disabilities Act (ADA), which protects people with disabilities from discrimination. We will send you a copy of her individualized 504 Plan after we all agree on it." I didn't want my daughter to be segregated at school, so I was glad that he was suggesting a plan that kept her in her homeroom.

After school, following a glass, or two, of wine, I took Imani out to ride her adapted tricycle. Brita, the girl next door who was one year older than Imani, and Hildegard's daughter, was out in her front yard playing with her brother, Martin.

"Why do you put her feet on like that?" she asked. It never bothered Imani when people stared or asked questions because she didn't know that it was considered rude. But Brita was a kid, so she didn't know better either.

"It's so they don't fall off," I explained.

"Why would they fall off?" Brita questioned.

"They just like to slide off," I told her.

"Mine don't slide off of MY bike and I can ride a TWO-wheel bike," she boasted.

"That's nice, and I'm glad you like your bike. Imani likes her trike, and we're going to go around the block now," I said as I pushed Imani away with the handle on the back.

We went through the neighborhood and said hello to kids and moms and dads and other neighbors as we went by. I walked fast because it was cold, but Imani wanted to go around twice. My hands were freezing.

When we got back, Hildegard was outside watching her kids play and going through her mail. She had a master's degree but had stopped working when she had kids. When I asked her about her background, which I compulsively asked everyone because I was still trying to learn about people outside of the church, she retorted sarcastically, "Do you want to see my curriculum vitae?" I cringed seeing her. She always did something belittling—like mocking people who smoked (like me) and looking at me up and down when I started gaining weight. She pushed the inferiority complex button in me. When she bragged about her career in law, I shrank because I hadn't finished college yet. And she flaunted her lifestyle, like how big her property was, where her apparently brilliant children went to *Montessori* school, and her enjoyable afternoons, as if to show me that I was nothing because I had none of these things. On my bad days, I was depressed over my incompetence, ugliness, poverty, and loneliness—away from her, where she couldn't see how much pain she inflicted.

Here she was with her perfect white picket fence life and she didn't know a damn thing about what I had going on. But she appeared to enjoy picking on me and going back into her house that was taken care of by her husband and her bimonthly cleaning lady. She didn't have homework at night or a toxic baby daddy or a job or a precarious living situation or half the problems I had. She had been privileged enough to establish herself academically and in her legal career before she was pregnant. When she talked about her former life, it was all lovely stuff. There was probably no church-prison or siblings she had to take care of or child molesters or uncle rapists in her life. She didn't need to drink or smoke or stay up late after her kids went to bed. She could read her magazines and relax and take naps in her hammock in the afternoon. One day of her life would have been a vacation to me. But I got no sympathy from her. She had to be miserable. Before you can stop hurting, you have to learn how to feel.

I went back inside and took two big shots of vodka to calm my nerves and forget fucking Hildegard. Then I went out back to have a cigarette and I didn't care if she saw me.

Charles' back yard looked so peaceful, and I wasn't. I shivered as I watched the smoke I exhaled, wishing it could take all of my anxiety with it. Just then, the kids came through the gate and shrieked that I was smoking, and I quickly crushed out my cigarette.

"Mom, Brita wants to try riding my trike," Imani said.

"Yeah, and I want you to strap my feet in," Brita requested.

"OK, be right there." I sighed.

For the next hour, the kids took turns riding Imani's trike, like the novelty that it was to them, until Hildegard called them in for dinner like a Queen summoning her subjects. I was chilled to the bone. I was ready to go inside, but her manner added to my resentment. Of course, she never thanked me for being the one to stay outside with the kids.

Charles was cooking pasta when we got in, and the kitchen smelled like red sauce and comfort.

"Can you make enough for her to take some for lunch tomorrow? She has a field trip." I asked him.

"Of course," he replied. "Are you all right?"

"Ugh, I hate that arrogant bitch next door," I huffed. "She thinks she's so important and she's just another housewife."

He looked at me sympathetically. "I think you have Hildegard syndrome and it's becoming an OCD thing."

Groaning, I agreed. "But I can't help it because she is SO. FUCKING. PATHETIC."

"If you think about it," he said, "she has no life, and this is how she gets her kicks, so she IS pathetic. It's pushing your buttons because on some level you believe her. But try not to put energy into that because you don't have any to spare."

He was right on this. If only I could stop letting her get under my skin. I ran my icy hands under warm water in the sink. My body ached, and I hoped I wasn't getting sick. Once Imani was back inside and we were sitting at the dinner table, me with a refilled wine glass, I started to shift gears.

Imani ate all of her pasta plus two pieces of garlic bread. It must have been the fresh air and exercise. I put leftovers into a Tupperware so she could take it to school for lunch the next day. Then it was time to read.

We sat on the sofa in the sunroom at the back of the house and started on the stack of books sitting on the glass coffee table. As my mother had done, I made the characters come to life with voices and sound effects. Imani loved it, just as I had. One of her favorite books was *Designed by God So I Must be Special,* even though it was tattered with splotches of food on it from when she was a baby. It was a book that celebrated how unique each of us is and how we are perfect as we are—that God doesn't make mistakes and He loves everyone, even unbelievers, though of course it didn't say that specifically.

"Imani, you are a special person and a beautiful, smart girl," I told her, tapping her on the nose.

She giggled and said, "I'm special like my mom!"

That night, I fell asleep in her bed as we snuggled and I woke up at 2:00 a.m. to do my homework.

* * *

My grades were in, and I had 3 A's and a B in my classes. I also made the Dean's List—how, I do not know. At Cubby's, it had been relatively quiet, and I was going to get a few weeks off from college. Christmas was around the corner.

* * *

Cubby had a lot of Christmas shopping to do: for his kids, his mother, his cousin, her husband, their kids, and a few friends. I got to his house at 9:00 a.m. instead of 10:00 a.m. so he could get a head start on it.

"Hey, big guy," I greeted him. "Are you ready to spend all your money today?"

"I'll be paying it off for the next six months." He laughed.

"Well, what do YOU want for Christmas?" I winked at him.

"How about 'Rock, Rhythm & Doo-Wop' that we saw on public television the other night?" he suggested.

"OK, but it's a secret," I teased.

I took a tissue and wiped his eyes and nose. Then I raised the head of his bed to get him in position to transfer into his wheelchair. "Boo!" I joked as he came near me, blowing him a kiss.

"I have to take a leak when I get in my chair," Cubby prompted me.

I swung his legs around so they were dangling over the side of his bed—then pulled him forward toward me into a hug. Together, locked in, we pivoted to his wheelchair and I sat him down slowly.

"Why can't everyone do it like you?" he said, shaking his head.

"They don't have twelve younger siblings and nursing school, silly," I said. "Not that you're a kid—because you're more like my grandpa—but I know how to do all of this care work."

"More like your GRANDPA?!" he shot back with feigned hurt, and then stiffened into a body spasm.

"You're the one naming your gray hairs when they fall out," I quipped as I waited for the spasm to pass.

He laughed, "Ha!" causing an additional spasm.

I brushed his beautiful, silver hair, parted exactly as he liked it, and we went into the kitchen to see what Gigi wanted and get ready for breakfast.

She was dancing to "Rocking Around the Christmas Tree" with a page in one hand and a pen in the other and chuckled heartily when she realized she had been discovered.

"You make life sparkle, Gigi," I complimented her.

For our special occasion that day, Cubby wore a Polo sweater—a blue one—and his good shoes. I put the sweater on after I brushed his teeth so we wouldn't spill on it.

"Do we have everything?" Cubby asked. "We need the urinal, wallet, disability parking tag, straws, and Baclofen."

"Um, let me see…yes, we have it all," I replied as I took an inventory of what Gigi had laid out on the hallway table in the entryway.

I went into the garage and opened the door. First, I had to move Gigi's 1989 Oldsmobile, aka "Bessie," into the guest spot so I could bring my car in. Before I had come over, I made sure my trunk was empty so there would be room for his wheelchair. His purchases could go in my back seat. Even though it was winter, I put the top down on my car because it was easier to transfer him into it that way.

"Easy does it!" I chimed as I lowered Cubby into my passenger seat. He started to spasm and shake, which made his legs stiffen up and clench. I pushed on them to stop the spasms and forced his legs to bend so I could slide them into my car while rotating his butt on the seat.

While Cubby warmed up in the car, I disassembled his wheelchair: took off the side cushions, unhooked the back and seat and pulled them off, swiveled the foot rests off and folded them, and collapsed the chair by yanking on the middle to fold it up. Then, each part had to go into my trunk—wheelchair first, followed by all of the smaller parts. By the time I was finished, my dry, chapped hands were like icicles.

"Bridge!" Cubby called. "I need you to scoot my butt back more." Positioning in the car was hard and not ergonomic—requiring bending at odd angles and pushing and pulling at those angles. Caregiving is one of the most dangerous jobs because of the high rate of injury, according to OSHA. Caregivers are exposed to infectious diseases and hurt their backs doing transfers and lifting, which can end their careers.

"It's all good; it's important that you're comfortable. You don't need to get any pressure sores on that cute golfer butt." Cubby had been an avid golfer and had golfed all over the world and at his country club. Now he played fantasy golf with his old golfing buddies—a playfully competitive game, with dirty jokes and occasional side bets.

"Do you want to listen to the oldies?" I asked Cubby as we started down the road. "Sure," he said.

Along the way, we went around corners and stopped at lights and stop signs. I supported and adjusted Cubby with my right hand. Otherwise he would slide around and his neck would fall forward. We had to look funny to people in other cars, because I would catch them looking at us as we pulled up to a red light with my hand on his forehead.

I found a parking spot at the Mall of America that had clear ground and enough room to do the transfer. Parking ramps made that easier because there was usually no snow or ice. The worst transfers were when I had on dress shoes for dinners out or their Christmas brunch at their country club and had to do the transfer on a slippery, snowy ground. One year, I did it in designer heels that I had found for $2.50 at a thrift store.

We browsed his favorite stores with home and kitchen merchandise and found a fancy wine opener, bar glasses, a CD, and a cheese basket for members of his family: Gigi and his cousin Karoline and her husband Ralph and sons. But he saved the big one for last: a Hooters calendar for Ralph, a human rights lawyer. This was a tradition each year, and

Ralph was extra delighted if the waitress, Spirit, had signed it, since she was his favorite.

I pushed Cubby and his squeaky wheelchair into Hooters and tried not to look at the girls. They were so much prettier than me, a washed-up old mom at twenty-five years old. I envied their confidence and freedom of expression.

"Hi, welcome to Hooters!" a thin, busty blonde chirped. "How can I help you today?"

Cubby told me to take the lead. "Um, hi. I guess he's looking for your calendar." My face flushed, and I couldn't make eye contact.

"Yeah, sure! Here you go. Is that all?"

"Well, if you could sign it, that would be great," I stammered. "You can just say: 'To Ralph, Stay Hot – Love, Spirit."

I looked at Cubby because I didn't know where else to look without appearing super awkward. My hands were sweaty and shaky, and I felt hot and dizzy. It was embarrassing to be a frumpy caregiver next to these glamorous girls and being complicit in gift giving that objectified young women, like me. I wanted to bolt out of there and hoped that nobody I knew had seen me.

She handed me the signed calendar with a Hooters girl on the front, and I hurriedly tried to stuff it into one of Cubby's other shopping bags, but they were all too small. So, I had to hold it until we got back to the car, so it wouldn't bend. It felt like everyone noticed that I was carrying this risqué item.

I pushed Cubby through the mall, bags hung on the handles of his wheelchair, sometimes rubbing against his tires, until we found the food court. Finally. We could sit down and rest, and I could get off of my aching feet and shake out my weary arms and hands.

"I think I want Chinese today," Cubby mused. "How about a chicken stir fry? You can get whatever you want."

We both got chicken stir fry. It seemed like a good idea, and I was too tired to think of anything else. I grabbed extra napkins to make a bib for Cubby and put a straw in his iced tea to give him a sip. Then I started scooping up the stir fry with a spoon to feed him. After I got him going, I could eat, and I was famished. I was also beat.

"I need to get home for my nap now," Cubby said.

Cubby took his time with many things, but he ate fast. He was almost done by the time I got a couple bites into my mouth. I quickly stuffed the rest of the meal into my mouth as my stomach growled.

When we got back to my car, I took a few slurps of cold coffee from my thermos. Sometimes I thought ahead, and my future self thanked me.

* * *

Back at home, Gigi was having a glass of wine on the sofa and visiting with her niece, Karoline. They were planning Christmas.

A half hour later, I had Cubby transferred and cozy in bed, and went back to the garage to get the gifts.

"Bridget, you're going to move my car back in, won't you?" Gigi asked.

"And make sure you don't block me in," Karoline said.

There was no thank you for what I had been doing all day for their family. There was only more work. Never-ending, thankless work.

"Yes," I said as I passed them in the living room. My legs barely cooperated with me to keep going.

I brought in the gifts and put them near the desk in the living room where all of the gifts were being stockpiled.

"You're coming back tonight, right?" Gigi asked me.

"Yes, in a couple hours," I replied.

"You're going to meet yourself coming and going," she joked.

Maybe she knew how I felt. She had to. Someone else had to.

* * *

On Christmas Eve, I worked at Cubby's during the day and then came back a couple hours earlier than I normally started my evening shift because his family was getting together at his house. In between, I dropped off Imani at Marcus' family party. At the end of the night, after Cubby's family went home around midnight, I again went to Marcus' party to pick up Imani.

When I got there, it was still in full swing. The house smelled like delicious food, and I could hardly hear above the din of chatter and laughter or see where Imani was in the sea of gifts and bodies. I craned my neck to scope out the room—looking for the colors of the Christmas dress I had put on her.

Marcus found me before I could find him. "Just sit down and chill. You're so annoying," I heard him say from behind me. I shrank into a chair, with no fight left in me. I wasn't sure how I was still awake as I sat with heavy, slumped shoulders. My hands were chapped raw, and my eyes were burning from exhaustion.

As I sat, I watched Marcus dote on Imani like he was a great father—attentive, caring, and patient. He was right there with her when she needed a hand and leaned in to hear every word from her mouth. It was a sight that I had always wanted to see, and it angered me because it was theatrical and vacuous, like a photo op. He wasn't this father who hugged and kissed his daughter to build her up and the doting father who made her days full and warm. Everything he did was for his own ego. I was angry that I had loved him and given my lovely child such a scumbag of a father.

It was almost 1:30 a.m. when we started loading Imani's many gifts into my car. She was still in party mode—high energy, merry, and chatty—and everyone was lamenting that she had to go home because they had missed her. I told them that she was usually free on weekends if they wanted to pick her up, but nobody acknowledged my offer.

The ride home was still, like "Silent Night." My window was cracked so I got cold air on my face to keep me from falling asleep at the wheel. Imani fell asleep within ten minutes.

Getting home was another unloading project. I had lost track of how many times I had loaded and unloaded people and their things today and throughout the holiday procession. But, carrying my beautiful, sleeping Christmas gift was literally like an ode to joy in the cold dark of night. Her tuckered out, almost elfish face, adrift in a dream, and pudgy red cheeks that still seemed to be laughing—well, that was everything.

Chapter 38: Not So Special

The school bus was filled to the brim with hyper elementary school kids who were bouncing around like atoms colliding. I stood behind Imani as she slowly ascended the bus stairs so I could help her if she needed it. She had gotten a new leg brace on the right side and no longer needed the short one on the left. It had a Bugs Bunny with a red strap—and she was proud of it because she had picked it out herself. We had gone shoe shopping after we went back to the doctor to pick it up and got matching red shoes with Velcro—a different size for each foot because the brace took up extra space. A 'lift' (a layer of sole) was added to the right one to compensate for the leg length discrepancy, since her smaller right leg was shorter.

Certain activities like stairs took her a little longer, and she needed a railing. I worried that people would get impatient while waiting for her to go at her pace and make her feel rushed—or worse, knock her over. So, I was glad that it was my spring break at college and I was able to take the time to go on this school fieldtrip.

When Imani got to the top of the stairs, a girl yelled, "Imani!" It was her friend Sydney, whom she had met and comforted with a piece of candy at orientation. They had become great friends and had regular playdates. Sydney was from a rich family who lived in a big house in one of the fancy neighborhoods, with a father who traveled around the world on business. Her mom was a nurse who worked every other Saturday.

Down the aisle Imani went, her blonde ponytail swaying from side to side. She scooted into the seat next to Sydney and held her brown bag lunch on her lap. I had packed it with a special surprise to brighten her day.

A few rows down, another mom motioned to me that I could sit next to her. Her name was Anna, and she lived in our neighborhood with her husband, who was an auto mechanic, and two daughters. She seemed a little gossipy, but she was pleasant and easier to talk to than most of the moms.

"Hey you!" she said. "How's college going?"

"It's going," I replied. "I have a year and a half left!"

"All right! I never went to college." She grinned. "Too busy living it up in the 80s and then I met Rick."

"I lived it up for about two months in the late 90s," I laughed. "That's how Imani happened."

She elbowed me playfully. "At least you had a little life before the grind of parenthood!"

"I guess you could say that," I said, making a silly face.

Anna then said, "It looks like Imani has a hard time with stairs. What's her issue again?"

I explained to her that I didn't usually talk about it because I tried to be more private, but I was fine with telling her because she was a friend. "She has cerebral palsy," I started. "That's why some physical activities are harder for her."

"Ohhhhh, I am so sorry," she said. "It's sad to see a beautiful girl handicapped."

But it wasn't sad, and there wasn't anything to be sorry about. Imani was full of life, feisty, caring, and curious. So what if she walked a little slow and wore a leg brace? That was merely a part of her, and I thought it made her unique, like her signature wit, love of animals, talent for painting, and way of charming everyone she met with her sassy brand of joy. Nothing about her made her less than anyone else. It was so strange when I heard these comments—because I knew her—the complete her.

"Are you serious right now?" I teased Anna, tilting my head and looking at her sideways. "I hope you know that the term 'handicapped' went out in the 80s like the Aqua Net-frozen bangs you wore during your hay day."

"Oh my gosh, I didn't mean it like that. I'm always putting my foot in my big mouth!" she said sheepishly. "I think all handicapped people are special."

"Hey," I said, "that's what a lot of people think, but it's old-school thinking now."

I continued and told her that we use the term "disability" instead of "handicapped" and that there is nothing sad or scary, or even inspirational, about disability. It's unfamiliar to a lot of people because disabled people have been hidden, marginalized, and segregated. And disability doesn't mean "broken" or that you want a cure—it was about managing the challenges and being accepted and having human rights. Of course, some people wanted a cure, like Cubby, because maybe they wanted to get back what they lost, and who could blame them? But most people wanted to belong and feel welcome and be supported to live a quality life like everyone else, regardless of whether or not they were able to work. I had been reading up since meeting with Imani's principal.

"And they're not special," I finished. "They're just people being people and living life. Disability is a normal thing—it's diversity—and everyone is an individual. We all have rights and deserve accessibility and inclusion in the community."

"Girl," she said, smiling. "That makes total sense now that you put it like that!"

"Yeah, I knew you would get it. My kid is your average six-year-old who doesn't eat her dinner and go to bed on time."

We both laughed. "Mom life," she said and gave me a high five. As a mom, I was a passionate advocate, but I hadn't reached the point of standing up for myself. I didn't even know how to practice self-care.

The conversation turned to neighborhood gossip about bitchy Hildegard and who was moving in and out. We agreed that we needed to get our girls together for a playdate.

Eventually, we ran out of topics and sat quietly. The kids had calmed down, too. I looked at the other moms who were on the fieldtrip: Haley's mom Susan, Tristan's mom Tammy, Charlie's mom Jeanette, and Brooke's mom Sheri.

Susan had a master's degree but didn't work anymore. Tammy was the president of the PTA, and her husband had a "good job." Jeanette was a classical musician like her husband. Sheri had a job, but I didn't know what it was, and her husband was a grocery store manager.

All the parents seemed light years ahead of me. They had houses and careers and organized families. Here I was staying with my much-older boyfriend, who people thought was my dad, in a wilted relationship, and Marcus, Imani's dad, was a criminal and deadbeat and I didn't know where he was living half the time. It still felt like I was a teenager on an extended timeline. Like I never did the whole growing up thing, but I got older anyway. Yet I tried to blend in, like doing a group dance you never practiced.

As I got to know the other parents, I started to appreciate them more. They loved their children and had a level of commitment to them that I could relate to. And they warmed up to me. Of course, we needed time to assess each other, being that we were from such different backgrounds. They weren't as old as I perceived them to be—but when I moved into the area, I was twenty-two, and they were thirtyish or more and had more of an air of my parents' ways than a kid a few years out of high school. A few of the moms now made small talk with me when I volunteered at school. Imani was welcomed into their homes, and they dropped their kids off at my house for playdates. I was starting to care less about our differences and gaps between our accomplishments. We were a community of parents, all of whom had dreams for their children. The dreams may have varied, but they all included happiness and success.

Once we arrived at the zoo, we all got into our groups. I was chaperoning six kids, including Imani. We all had a great time looking at all the animals and eating our lunches together. Imani found her surprise from me: a picture I drew of her next to a tiger because that was one of her favorite animals.

Our ride back to school was more subdued, and a couple of the kids fell asleep. I sat with a kid who was feeling sick in the front of the bus.

I drove Imani home from school that day, and she told me that it was fun having me there. She flopped down on the couch in the sunroom to watch television, and I stretched her legs. The conversation with Anna replayed in my head like a broken record. It was disturbing that she had believed in what she was saying, convinced that she was being a nice person. I was appalled by her ableism. She was a friend and very open to hearing me. I thought about all the people who didn't have a personal connection to disability that led to forward thinking. We often don't have insight about something until we have a personal experience with it—and even then, sometimes people still get it wrong, yet think they are experts on it overall. Attitudes were a tough barrier. I didn't want "positive thinking"; I wanted empathetic listening and expanded thinking that humanized people. Getting through to them would be much tougher, and they were going to be people that Imani would encounter in the community. Something had to be done to change this.

* * *

On a winter day with a few inches of snow on the ground, I was doing homework at the kitchen table when I saw the bus pull up to the corner. I had been so wrapped up with my assignment that I forgot to get to the bus stop to wait for Imani. Quickly, I saved the paper I was writing for my Shakespeare class.

Glancing again out the window, I noticed that she was making her way down the street, limping, with her red Lands End boots that were not completely Velcroed shut and tufts of blonde pigtails sticking out of her bright blue knit hat. Someday, I thought, I would apologize to her for anything I possibly could have done wrong during my pregnancy to cause her to live with disability and all the struggles that went with it—like people staring at her and asking invasive questions about her legs, and people treating her differently and like she was less.

But I couldn't say anything today because I didn't want to confuse her or make her think that there was anything wrong with how she walked, or her body. Of course, I thought that she was perfect the way she was and I wouldn't change anything. It was the world that I was worried about. A world that I knew all too well. Discrimination does not always look like hate. Sometimes it looks like love.

Cramming my feet into my boots and whipping on my winter jacket, I went out through the garage and shuffled briskly down the driveway.

When I got to the end, she was already almost there. "Imaaaaani!" I cheered, extending my arms to welcome her with a hug.

"Mom! We had a snowball fight at school at recess! My mittens are still wet, and my hands are cold," she divulged.

I pulled off her mittens, put them in my jacket pocket, and held my warm hands over her ice-cold ones. "Let's go inside so you can warm up," I said.

Inside, I helped her remove her winter gear and pull her right leg that wore a brace out of her boot since it was wedged in tightly.

Once I hung up her winter gear, I checked to see if her clothes were wet from playing in the snow. Her socks were damp, and the bottoms of her jeans were soaked. We went upstairs to her bedroom to get her changed into dry clothes. Today she had worn a pair of jeans that I had bought her when we did back-to-school shopping. They were from Limited Too at the mall, and they had flower detailing. They were a little expensive, but it was our only big shopping trip of the year, when I got my student loan. Besides, I wanted her to fit in at school where many of the children came from affluent families with big houses and nice cars and could afford vacations and trendy things. Every morning, I continued to dress her up with a cute outfit, accessories, and hairstyle. I also did my best to buy cute shoes and not the old-school clunky orthotic shoes that would make her stand out.

"Mom, a boy at school asked me why I walk funny," she said as I put on her dry socks.

"Oh? What did you tell him?" I asked, hoping it didn't chip away at her sweet little heart.

"I said it's like a dance that tells part of my story," she said proudly, standing tall.

"Wonderful," I laughed with delight, tapping her on the nose.

Chapter 39: Regalia

Trudging through the snow from the daycare parking lot where I paid $50 per month to park during my last year of college, I carried a spiral-bound hard copy of my thesis: "The Effects of Sibling Behavior on Antisocial and Aggressive Attitudes." This was to be the conclusion of my work as a research assistant/behavior coder with the Minnesota Center for Twin & Family Research, which studies genetic and environmental influences on psychology.

My research provided a context for helping me understand the dynamics in my own family—why we clashed at times or how we related. I also discovered that we are not as in control of our behavior as we would assume and we are shaped by a variety of factors, including very powerful conditioning, such as that I received from the church. The church had limited me from functioning outside of it, and I had few skills to live independently and cope with life. I didn't have a well-formed identity, and I had a deep lack of experience in mainstream culture. Because I was disempowered by my religion of origin, I was vulnerable. This led to being taken advantage of and finding myself in dangerous situations. Ultimately, I sought anything that looked like security and comfort, although much of it did not serve me and was not in my best interest. My parents had complied with their church and hadn't protected me. When I told my dad that his older brother had raped me, he said, "I told you not to go with him." Like I would've listened when we had no trust—and it was never my fault, no matter what the circumstances were. And when I tried to open up about my childhood pain, my mom and dad's initial reaction was to be dismissive of me. Their false sense of loyalty was to an imaginary god, to the detriment of their very real daughter. I could never count on them while they followed their cultish religion. I was never a priority. I was a spiritual orphan and so was my daughter—it was cycle.

My education had opened up my awareness far beyond the sheltered confines of the church. I had stretched and expanded intellectually and delved into subjects I had never heard of. My brain had not only wriggled its way out of a psychological prison like a magician escaping from his locks under water but had proven to me that it was possible to thrive in unfamiliar worlds.

My advisor, Professor Becker, had just returned from doing research in Europe and emailed me a time to meet him at his office. I pushed the button on the elevator in Elliott Hall and remembered all the times I had gone up to the fourth floor for my research assistant job to code behaviors of research participants on video tapes. The elevator opened, and I went in, clutching my thesis—my own personal Bible because it signified my victory and personal resurrection from Hell. It honored the little girl in me who was passionate about learning and dreamed of success. After everything, I still came out on top and proved a lot of people wrong about me. Professor Becker was one of the many people who helped me make that happen. He was passionate about his students and had an unassuming presence that made him less intimidating, even though he was famous for his breakthrough research in his field.

"Professor Becker?" I asked quietly, so as not to disturb him, as he was clearly very focused on what he was doing on his computer.

Instantly, he looked up—then smiled softly. "Oh, hello, Bridget. So good to see you. Come on in."

I pulled my backpack off and sat in a chair next to his desk. "Here's my thesis," I said as I handed it to him. He had already graded it, and this was the last formality. "Thank you for being so great, and all your guidance. It means a lot."

"Of course," he remarked, like it was no big deal that he had been communicating with me for the past year, including while he was traveling abroad. "You did very well."

"Well, I never knew I could write this much until this project, so it was a good challenge. I've been thinking about going to grad school," I informed him.

"You certainly could," he affirmed. "I think you should keep up your writing and find jobs that allow you to keep growing. And let me know if I can be a reference for you. You were one of my most determined students and you have a lot of potential."

I was elated but tried to keep my composure. "That is incredibly kind; thank you, Professor Becker."

We shared a smile, and I told him I would let him get back to work. I couldn't stop smiling, and my face flushed with pride.

I remembered Dr. Thompson, Imani's NICU doctor, who was a professor in the medical school and how he had connected me with Dr. Marino, a researcher at the first study I worked for: the Laboratory for Human Developmental Psychobiology, which had ultimately had led me to Professor Becker. Dr. Thompson told me that they "help the beautiful and brilliant survive" when I emailed him about Imani being in elementary school and told him that I was a University of Minnesota student. Then he encouraged me to do research and emailed Dr. Marino to introduce and speak highly of me.

Driving home that afternoon in my gold convertible, I listened to one of my lyrical mantras: Reba McEntire's "Fancy." I sang it at the top of my lungs as chills went through my whole body. Fancy was a poor girl who left home and entertained men and made something of herself in the bigger world.

* * *

My grades were in—the last grades in over eleven years of striving to get my B.A. I made summa cum laude Latin honors, plus distinction!

"Gaaahhhh!" I shrieked when I read my final cumulative GPA and saw that I had gotten it by .03. I sat and stared at it on my computer, clicking and clicking to refresh the screen. But it was still the same. By a hair, I had crossed the threshold to enter the elite club of college graduates.

When I had started college, I was fifteen years old and wrote my papers long hand or with a typewriter. I drove a $500 car that I had to get into by climbing across the passenger seat. I was in the church and didn't smoke or drink, and the most rebellious thing I did was go to a movie with other "wild" church kids—after scoping out the parking lot to make sure we didn't get busted by a church spy.

When my life took a sharp turn and I found myself battling poverty and the adversities of single parenthood, I never gave up on my dream of getting my education. In my classes, I met people who inspired me, and through my life experiences, I learned about myself and the depths of what I was capable of. A professor had looked me in the face and told me how tenacious I was, and I said fiercely that I didn't want to live the alternative. But my dreams had become tempered with an appreciation for difficulty. I gained insight into how tough the world is. Yet, I would keep pushing boundaries. My own and others'. Now that I had achieved my dream and received my degree, perhaps I would have a career that would not only make a difference for others but also bring more security and abundance into my life.

When Imani's bus pulled up to the corner that day, I was already there, almost jumping out of my skin in anticipation of telling her my news. She went down the stairs, one at a time, like every afternoon, with flushed cheeks and dancing eyes. Shuffling toward me in her bright yellow (much like the hue of the paper suns I decorated my first apartment with) winter jacket, her face lit up to see me waiting for her. "Mommy!" she cheered as she hugged me around the waist, burying her face into my warmth.

"Imani, Mommy is done with college! You get to see Mommy graduate at the University of Minnesota!" I announced.

"Wow, Mommy, good job!" she exclaimed, bouncing up and down. She was my number one fan.

Hildegard stood in her yard staring at me while her three kids ran around and she looked too weary to deal with them. My life had grown, and she wasn't important—she was never actually relevant. I didn't give two shits.

* * *

At graduation, Imani was the first person I saw when I turned to exit the stage down the stairs—her beaming, nearly laughing with exuberance, beautiful little face. And next to her were Cubby, Charles, and my parents. My mom took a picture of me as I held up my degree, wearing my honors regalia. Flash!

* * *

That weekend, Imani and I visited my family. "Do you girls want to go to church tomorrow morning?" my mom asked Imani and me as she cooked spaghetti on the stove. The kitchen smelled like the garlic bread that was baking in the oven. I agreed to go because I wanted to stay in touch with my relatives in the church and felt strong enough to be in that environment again.

We arrived a few minutes late and the chorus of "A Mighty Fortress is Our God" accompanied by the pipe organ greeted me, as well as hushed "God's Peace" exchanged among the church members who were still filing into the sanctuary. I opened the familiar door with the same rickety push bar that had always been there. For a moment, I paused to recall how far my life had taken me since I had fled this church. I had been a different person then—younger, fearful, and obedient, but full of fire to be free. And yet, I still worried about what they thought of me. There were a few links left on the chain of my old bondage.

Since the main sanctuary was full, I walked Imani into the "overflow" area, where people went when they were late or if their kids were acting up or they wanted to be in a less formal space where they could come and go more easily and talk without getting the attention of the entire sanctuary. As we proceeded through the lobby of the church, a few "believers" instinctively turned around in their benches to look at us. I smiled awkwardly at them, trying to show them that I was happy away from there—that I didn't need them to be fine. When we opened the doors to the overflow room, we came face to face with dozens of "believers" who had heard rumors about me and bent their heads together to gossip. I straightened my shoulders and walked to a row of open seats, clutching Imani's little fat hand. She stopped momentarily to pick up a penny on the floor, and I waited with agonizing patience to get us seated, feeling on display as I stood there. The silence was uncomfortable, and I passed the time during the sermon by playing with Imani's hair, like the other young moms and older sisters did—like I had done before with my younger sisters and kids that I borrowed to occupy my time. I helped Imani color in a church coloring book so we both would have something to do. Then I French-braided her hair and put a clip from my purse at the end to hold it. Discretely, I looked around the room to see if I recognized anyone. A few of my cousins were there, but not sitting together. Most of the children sat with their peers from their Sunday school class if they weren't with their parents or taking care of children. One of my old friends sat with her three children and shunned my gaze. She had become important because her husband was one of the ministers.

Church ended with the last verse of "Children of Thy Heavenly Father."

I remembered singing that hymn as a young girl and believing in its lyrics. There was so much that I realized that I missed about the church since running away from it: the community, traditions, familiarity, and sense of security.

Family. I remembered why it was painful to leave and why I grieved when I didn't go back. Everything I had known was here.

With the last note the pipe organ uttered, I took Imani by the hand and hastened her to the main sanctuary to where my parents were sitting in the front row. As we approached, I soaked in the image of them and nine of their thirteen children. They took up half of the first row with their younger kids and the older ones were behind them in the second row. Within the first few seconds of church ending, the kids started to move around and scatter but stayed within range of our mom and dad because we needed permission to go anywhere.

I thought about how my parents and siblings were restricted to an invisible jail cell that they believed they lived in willingly. This made me feel both sad and guilty—guilty that I had wriggled my way free. My only consolation was they seemed to be happy with their lot in life, not knowing anything else.

"Time to go, you two," I teased my parents.

"Yeah, Grandma and Grandpa, you're not listening," Imani said, following along with me.

My parents both laughed. They were talking to one of the ministers and his wife, who had come from Finland years before.

"Sorry to interrupt," I apologized.

"It's fine, Bridget," Kaija, the minister's wife, said. "It's nice to see you back at church today. I know your parents have had a hard time with you away from here and having a child out of wedlock. They were disappointed. But all children are a gift from God."

I laughed nervously. "I've been through a lot, too," I said. As sad as my parents may have been for losing me, they didn't show it. They continued to be hard on me and this deepened my sense of abandonment and being judged.

"God wants you to honor your parents," Kaija continued. "You are supposed to obey them." I was almost thirty years old. THIRTY.

I didn't know what to say and turned my attention to what the kids were doing. Imani was playing around with my youngest brothers and climbing up and down the pulpit, even though it was sacred and they weren't supposed to be up there. It occurred to me that Kaija was looking out for my parents because they had lost me, and because the church had, too. It was all about other people and not about me.

We did the "Minnesota Goodbye" and took a half hour to chat with people as we made our way to the lobby and parking lot. My parents and siblings piled into their van. Instead of a ritual of leaving with my friends, as I had done in the last chapter of my church life, I packed up my daughter and buckled her into her car seat.

Back at my parents' house, we got lunch ready. I cut a head of lettuce for a salad. My dad put a pan of day-old bread he had picked up from the church kitchen in the oven—a donation from a bakery owned by a church family. "Do you girls want some bread?" he asked.

"Yeah!" Imani and I both said at the same time, and then laughed because we did that a lot.

"Ah, you two. You are like twins! Imani is a little Bridgie through and through." Mom chuckled, as though she was reminiscing on her favorite days with me when I was young—before my rebellion and mental health breakdowns, and subsequent sharp exit from all she and my dad had tried to instill in me. It was as if she held onto the dream of what she wished for my life, not unlike my adherence to my dreams for my own daughter. We looked at each other, and I saw her own inner child flash across her face—the one I had only heard about in stories from her mother—the little shy girl with piercing blue eyes and soft brown hair and a precociousness she had bequeathed to me and I to Imani. Worlds apart, we were still cut from the same cloth—like two paper suns.

"We got it from our mama," I said.

"Ha! I've made so many mistakes," Mom said. "Being a mom is hard, and I would do many things differently."

"Well, that's just humility," I consoled her, and not for the first time. "How in the world you got married right out of high school and then had a baby practically every year—dang, woman, you are a tough cookie."

"Yes, she is," Dad said as he drifted slowly up the stairs with a cake from church. "The Mom is the one who keeps everything running." Once in the kitchen, he kissed Mom as she stirred spaghetti sauce into the noodles and told her she was beautiful. They had a kind of love I had always wanted—affectionate, loyal, and committed. They had been through job losses, poverty, Mom's four years of college with a couple more babies in the process, miscarriages, their precious firstborn rejecting the life they had built, a grandchild out of wedlock, health scares, and difficult family dynamics with their own parents and siblings. And yet, the first thing they did when they saw each other was kiss like they meant it. I wondered if I would ever feel like that with someone and at the same time was skeptical if they had settled for a boring provincial life because they knew no better. There had to be a balance in there somewhere—a sweet life with someone you loved who made you feel free.

Chapter 40: Walking Backwards

When Imani was eight years old, she was scheduled for her first orthopedic surgery on both legs—specifically, "bilateral femoral derotational osteotomies with a slight shortening on left, a right Strayer, and right hamstring and gastrocnemius botox." This meant that both large leg bones would be cut, rotated, and pinned because her thigh bones were now abnormally rotated inward due to cerebral palsy. Some bone would be trimmed from the left femur to even it out with her right leg. Muscle adjustments would be made to the right leg, and botox injections would be administered to the tight muscles in the right leg to loosen them up.

All of this would place Imani's legs in proper alignment and improve her gait. After rehabilitation, including a lot of physical therapy, it looked like she might be able to say goodbye to wearing a leg brace. It was too soon to make that call, but we believed there would be dramatic results in her mobility. Imani told her surgeon to put her legs on backwards and she would invite her to her dance party afterward.

* * *

Six days after the surgery, Imani was ready to go home. I stripped the sheets off the small foldout couch and the pillow cases off the stiff pillows in her room and packed our bags. The parade of professionals visited her hospital room to sign off on her discharge plans and provide instructions for the coming days and weeks. She wore knee immobilizers on both legs to keep them in alignment, and a rental wheelchair was delivered to her room with a folder of paperwork. Luckily, she didn't need a partial body cast because her metal hardware was so secure, and she got away with a short cast on her right leg.

***

Back at home, we enjoyed the lazy days of summer when I wasn't working at Cubby's. I stockpiled the sun room, where Imani camped out, with books, games, and toys to keep her occupied.

Carefully, I slid her knee immobilizers underneath her legs, without moving them, and strapped them securely. "OK, honey, I'm going to pick you up now," I said. She grabbed me around the neck, and I scooped her up with one arm under her knees and one around her waist. She was only about fifty pounds, and I was used to lifting Cubby, who was over two hundred pounds. I carried her outside through the front door and down four steps to her wheelchair, which was sitting on the front walk with the leg rests up. After she was settled, I put on a light fleece blanket that she had made during crafts at the hospital by tying the fringes together. She had also painted a birdhouse and planted seeds in a plastic cup. And she made a few friends with other kids who had surgeries and other procedures—some who were going to be in the hospital for months.

We went around the block and talked to her friends who were playing outside. This was our first day out. She didn't seem to mind that she couldn't be on the ground with them, drawing with chalk on the driveways, or running through the sprinkler. They were a welcome sight, nonetheless.

"Thank you for signing my get well poster!" Imani called to Brita, who was riding her bike toward us. Brita sped up and swerved around her, and both of them erupted into giggles.

"You're welcome," Brita said. "Do I get to sign your cast, too?" There were a few signatures on it already from staff, friends, and visitors at the hospital.

"Yeah, go get a marker!" Imani said eagerly. Brita ran off and we kept walking.

"Isn't this a nice break from the sun room?" I asked Imani. It was a relief to see her so happy after going through such a major surgery. I hoped she would get through this unscathed and be done with braces and therapies, and her medical issues could be in the past. This would alleviate some of my guilt, as well, since part of me still blamed myself for her being born premature, even though my sister Claire also had a premature child now. She was still in the church and had a husband and typical life—and her baby had been born a month earlier than Imani. Apparently, our lifestyles were inconsequential, though the adversity and difficult environment didn't help my pregnancy.

When my niece Hannah was born, I stopped explaining to people why I thought Imani was born early—that it could have been stress from Marcus or pollution or lifting heavy people at work, or maybe I hadn't quit drinking soon enough. Something compelled me to analyze her birth and delivery like I was repenting for my sins, though my doctors cited no known cause except a possible "incompetent cervix." Claire had researched what happened in her case and found genetic theories for her preterm birth. We were the only two sisters who had children, so time would tell if our other sisters had complications.

Imani's friend Sara's dog barked at us as we approached her house. Imani was slightly reclined in her wheelchair, and her arms were loosely draped over the armrests. She looked more like she was lounging on a lawn chair at the beach. The front door flung open, and blonde, curly-haired Sara dashed across her lawn with her arms open.

"Imani! Yay!" she cried. The girls hugged and laughed at seeing each other again after a week. "Are you going to fireworks for the fourth of July?" Sara asked.

Sara's mother and I talked about summer plans and said that the girls should have playdates. However, the next week, we would be at my parents' to spend time with them and give Imani a diversion. A few of the older kids had moved out, and there were still about ten at home. They were waiting for us and had already promised Imani the coveted big reclining sofa in the living room. The house was not wheelchair accessible, but I could carry Imani up and down the stairs and have one of the kids carry the disassembled wheelchair. She would have enough space to do her physical therapy exercises ("range-of-motion") on the floor to stay limber until she could bear weight and start walking again. In a couple weeks, we would be going to her friend Kendall's cabin. Our social calendar was nearly full for the summer.

As would be expected, Imani was determined to recover and sometimes went a little too fast with her walker. One day, after seeing *Pirates of the Caribbean 2,* she said, "I'm going to do a stunt. I'm going to go off this curb! It'll be like walking the plank!"

Marcus stopped calling or trying to see Imani after she left the hospital, but it was just as well. He lectured the both of us on the importance of Imani "overcoming" her disability and trying harder. According to him, she was lazy, and I was soft. We didn't take his calls, and didn't need to, and had a wonderful summer!

I set up accommodations through the nurse and teachers so Imani could go back to school while she was still doing rehabilitation, which would last for up to a year. She got a bus service with a paraprofessional who helped her get to and from school.

* * *

One morning after many conversations about playing violin, the bus driver, Carl, handed Imani a printout about Itzhak Perlman, a famous Israeli-American violin virtuoso who had polio when he was four-years-old and became a disability advocate as well, with a focus on accessibility.

"He is partially paralyzed and gets around with crutches and wheels like you," he said with a big, radiant grin. "He has adapted quite well, and I thought you would like to learn about him."

Then he shook my hand and told me I had a lovely daughter. With people like him, the world could be a more inclusive place for my sweet girl. I grabbed his strong, gentle hand and held it for a moment before letting go.

Chapter 41: What I Promised Myself

When I was adjusting to my new life as a teen single mom and the weight of my responsibilities was heaviest, I had promised myself that, one day, I would use my experiences to make a difference for others and pass on what I had learned from Imani and others I cared for and loved so that fewer people would suffer. When Imani was eight years old, I was given the opportunity to fulfill it. It started with Joe.

Joe's apartment was quiet when I walked in, and I didn't see him anywhere. So, I looked around. Then I heard a quiet, unintelligible voice from the bedroom and went to the doorway. There was a dresser piled with Gopher spirit wear and an open closet, organized by color. But there was no Joe to be found.

"Joe?" I asked timidly, hoping I was in the right place.

"Yeah," I heard a muffled voice say.

"Where are you?" I asked, scanning the room, baffled by the empty bed. He called again, and it came from the direction of his bed.

"Joe, I don't see you," I apologized.

With a strained effort to speak and raise his voice, I heard him say, "Floor!"

Bending down, I scanned the room again and spotted a bundle of blankets on the floor behind his bed near the wall.

Walking around to the side of his bed that was next to the wall, I saw his face, poking out from tangled up blankets.

"Oh my God! Joe, are you OK? What should I do?" I gasped, rushing over to him.

Joe laughed and said, "I was practicing some acrobatics and missed my mark. You can get me up, but be careful because I have a neck brace on."

He was thin and bony, and it was easy to lift up his light body and put it back in bed. I straightened out his blankets and put a pillow under his neck by pulling him up by the shoulders. Everything Joe needed was connected to the bed railing with some kind of strap or cord: television remote control, bed control, water bottle, and phone.

"Well, geez," Joe said with a laughing smile after getting situated. "What an introduction. I'm Joe, by the way."

His agency, where I worked part-time, had called me because his regular PCA hadn't shown up. Joe told me that he worked at the University of Minnesota as a researcher and that he was taking a medical leave to recover from surgery after falling and sustaining a spinal cord injury. He had tripped on a rug at his townhouse while rushing off to work. For years, people had told him to get a wheelchair because his walking was so unsteady (due to cerebral palsy), but he refused. "I wanted to be a regular guy," he said.

The timing of his accident was highly inconvenient, as he was preparing to work on his dissertation to complete his Ph.D. Unfortunately, that had to be put on hold. He moved into a student apartment building and a lot of the other students helped him out part-time, with the hope that he could get back to walking and driving, and, of course, working, again. Back to his life.

Joe and I became fast friends as we worked together, and like Cubby, he became an important mentor in my life—as well as Imani's. Joe loved folk music, public radio, and U of M sports and was one of the funniest people I'd ever met. He liked shaving after his shower and putting gel in his hair and took a long time getting ready, so I nicknamed him "Metrosexual." He nicknamed me "Radical Finn."

Joe had won awards for his contributions to the disability community over the course of his career: one from Courage Center, where Imani had gone for therapies—and then a "Charlie Smith Award" from the disability community newspaper Access Press. He invited me to attend the ceremonies with him.

At the Charlie Smith Award event, I made a short speech honoring Joe. Gigi and Cubby had given me advice on how to dress for the event: a pink cashmere sweater that Gigi had given me for Christmas and a wool skirt that Cubby picked out for me when I took him shopping with his daughter.

There were players from the disability community at both events. But I was there for Joe and had no agenda; I didn't even know about the "disability community."

At the Courage Center event, I met Jake Harding from the University of Minnesota Institute on Community Integration, a research institute focused on disability. He told me about the Direct Support Professional Association of Minnesota (DSPAM)—an organization that advocates for caregivers like me. It was a state chapter of the National Alliance for Direct Support Professionals (NADSP). The mission was to strengthen the direct support workforce that empowers disabled people to live their own lives in the community. He encouraged me to come to their meetings because they wanted people doing disability services to use their knowledge to make services better.

Over the years, I had heard about organizations and programs that were focused on the disabled. However, they seemed segregated ("special") to me and I wanted Imani to have a regular life and not be separated from everyone else. I wanted my daughter to be treated like a normal person, and not like she was "special."

Over the next few months, I continued speaking with Jake about DSPAM and learned of its work to advocate for direct support professionals: higher wages, more respect, affordable healthcare, and career pathways. He asked me to be a candidate for the Direct Support Professional Association of Minnesota board of directors. By this time, I was a lifelong veteran of the disability workforce, having been both a personal care assistant and family caregiver. Other candidates were well-known leaders, but I was elected to give voice to direct support professionals.

* * *

A few weeks after I was elected, we had a board meeting and discussed who would be the new board officers. I volunteered to take notes after someone told me what "minutes" were.

Carol Scott, a co-director of Advocating Change Together, looked at me with confidence and said, "I think that Bridget Siljander would be an excellent choice for president and chair of the board because she has been a PCA for so many years and Joe clearly loves her. She's smart and kind and has shown a lot of enthusiasm for this organization. I'll mentor her if she's interested." I watched her say these words in amazement because I knew that I was getting my chance to be a leader and stand up for others, and myself.

With my position on the board, I could affect change by using it as a platform to address the systemic workforce issues. It wasn't very clear how I would do that yet, but I sensed that I could be a spokesperson from the trenches and fight for our cause.

I kept Joe and Cubby updated on these exciting developments—how I had been learning about the basics of advocacy, disability history, running meetings, going to trainings and conferences, and meeting leaders in the direct support movement. I called myself a "direct support professional" now because advocates wanted to use one term to unify us.

* * *

"Hello, Madame Chair," Cubby said proudly one morning. "Tell me your latest good news." I showed him a newspaper article about "caregivers" and the care crisis that Gigi had clipped out of the newspaper and put on the table in the front hallway.

"We need a lot more people like me to be available for people like you, Cubby," I said. "We aren't the only ones in this situation."

"You are exactly right," he reflected. "If it weren't for you, I would still be in a nursing home, if I had lived long enough. I can't imagine my life without you. I really can't."

"You are worth it," I beamed.

My world as an advocate kept expanding. I was offered a contract job as a curriculum author at the University of Minnesota Institute on Community Integration and began writing courses on how to support people with physical disabilities in the home and community—for a national curriculum library called College of Direct Support. I was honored that I could capture so much of my industry knowledge to share with other direct support professionals and utilize my research and writing skills from my education to develop quality trainings.

Then I was selected to attend a leadership program called the Voices Institute through the Direct Care Alliance, a national nonprofit organization in New York City that empowered "direct care workers," as they called them, to organize and build a movement to affect change through collaboration. Afterward, I was hired as the Voices Institute Coordinator.

Still, I worked split shifts with Cubby and managed Imani's life. It was exciting but overwhelming, and I couldn't wait to work just one job.

My email signature read:

Direct Support Professional
Direct Support Professional Association of Minnesota, President and Chair
Direct Care Alliance, Voices Institute Coordinator
University of Minnesota Institute on Community Integration, Curriculum Author

* * *

"How's my favorite fourth grader?" I asked Imani cheerfully when I got home from a board meeting, putting down my briefcase. We had been living in our own apartment for about a year. Charles had protected us, even if he was a curmudgeon to live with at times, and now I was sure I could protect Imani and myself. I had moved on from him with confidence. Men were never going to save me, and water couldn't be turned into wine.

Imani was ten years old, and I remembered being ten. I was a sister-mom and babysat for all the church families in the neighborhood and had a savings account. At the time, I felt all grown up. Imani still seemed like my little girl.

"I'm playing a computer game—Webkinz!" she said.

"You climbed up on that chair?" I asked, anxious that she could have been hurt while I was gone.

"Silly mommy, of course, I did. I just fell and hit my head a few times," she said wryly.

"You stinker," I said. "Next time, use the step stool, OK?"

I told Imani about the board meeting and was proud that she had a mother who was a leader—tired, but a leader, nonetheless.

Chapter 42: Letter in a Bottle

Uncle Harold tried to contact me on Facebook. He had read all about me on Google, about my work in the disability community, and said, "My, you've been busy."

"I know you're disappointed that the police didn't move forward on your case because the statute of limitations expired, but there are many ways you can get justice," my therapist said.

"Like how?" I asked, hoping it would be something that would make me feel vindicated.

"Well, for one, you didn't turn out like him. So, you transcended a significant amount of your pain and trauma by maintaining your integrity," she went on. I realized that kindness is a form of justice, even though I was still angry.

I let her words marinate in my thoughts for a few moments. Then I felt a surge of pride that I had led a life I could look back on with satisfaction. "You know what? I like that," I said.

I decided to write Harold a letter.

Harold,

I did not write back to you before because I was not ready to communicate with you. But now I am. First of all, you did things to me that you never should've done. Those things have caused me a lifetime of suffering that I never deserved, and I want you to know about the damage. You shattered my trust in people and my sense of safety. I expected you to be my uncle. Now I will spend the rest of my life trying to heal and stop the memories from haunting me. It has taken me to hell and back to get to this point. Your momentary pleasure destroyed me. I know you have done this to other girls because I have talked to them, so your behavior is not a secret—although much of the family is still in denial about what a monster you are. The trauma has set me up to be caught in a cycle of abuse. And I know you picked me because you thought I was weak. Now I'm holding you accountable, and although it took me a while, I am no longer silent. I've had to be the strong one and say I'm not living in shame anymore. And I've had to be the one that tried to bring some justice, even after all the trauma I've been through and how much it has broken me. Finally I feel like I don't have to justify my pain. This would be a different letter if you had tried at some point over the many years to seek forgiveness and redemption and shown that you wanted to change yourself and how our culture treats women. You could have reflected on the impact of your actions and apologized. You could have done so many things that you failed to do. I am telling you the truth and I know you may not want to hear it, but that doesn't change it. You were wrong to violate me, and you are wrong for refusing to own that. Finally, stop contacting me and trying to be in my life. I owe you nothing.

I never sent this letter. It felt almost pointless because he never made an effort to be a better person. Looking at his Facebook page, I read posts and comments disparaging women who were feminist or stood up to men. He complained about how they ruined men's lives. He was a raging Republican—the kind that Cubby despised. But the very act of writing it made me feel like I was taking back some of my power from him. My personal power was built on the foundation of giving power to others and the joy of connecting with them—people like my daughter and Cubby and Joe—so they could live a better life and be who they wanted to be.

Chapter 43: I Am the Face and Voice

On February 11, 2009, I testified before the Minnesota Senate Health and Human Services Budget Division at the State Capitol. My daughter was in my heart, along with friends and family and all the people I had provided care and support to over the years. I was also testifying for my past self. I had seen how disabled people lived and were treated. We deserved better lives, so I took that microphone and preached.

Good morning, Madame Chair and Committee Members. My name is Bridget Siljander. I am the face and voice of one of tens of thousands of caregivers in Minnesota. I am a Personal Care Assistant (PCA), the President of the Direct Support Professional Association of Minnesota (DSPAM), and the mother of a child who has cerebral palsy. I hold a bachelor's degree in psychology, summa cum laude, from the University of Minnesota.

DSPAM is opposed to a number of the Governor's recommended budget cuts to Disability Services and PCA services.

You probably won't see many of our faces or hear many of our voices because we are a marginalized and underrepresented workforce. DSPAM members believe that the PCA program can't afford cuts and PCAs can't afford reductions to their wages.

As a PCA for over ten years, I have barely survived on my wages while working numerous split shifts over the course of exhaustingly long work days, and spending hours daily in my car driving between consumers, sometimes up to four hours per day. Though I toiled, and for a period of two years, worked split shifts seven days per week, I still needed subsidized housing, public assistance benefits, trips to the food shelf, and Minnesota Care and Medicaid for myself and my daughter.

It was humiliating for someone who prides herself on her self-sufficiency. I didn't like getting public assistance. In fact, I hated it. But, I was forced to make up for the gap between my earnings and the basic cost of living. I recall many times when preparing food for a consumer that I wished I could afford groceries. I want you to know that I am proud of my work ethic and of the standard of service that I provide. I am good at what I do and through my advocacy, I am raising awareness that this work demands intelligence, talent, skill, independence, and problem-solving abilities.

The Governor's Recommendation cuts more than $85 million in Fee-for-Service PCA Services over two years, over the next biennium. These dollars will be removed from the economy. Since this industry is highly labor-intensive, many of these dollars will be taken out of the pockets of PCAs and other DSPs—people already struggling to pay for transportation, housing, food, utilities, and healthcare—people who put their dollars right back into their local communities. This seems contrary to efforts to stimulate the economy, empower individuals, and support each other.

DSPAM opposes the governor's recommendation to eliminate eligibility for MinnesotaCare, GAMC hospital only, and transitional MinnesotaCare for adults without children. Because DSPs are low-wage workers, are more likely to take advantage of Medicaid-funded health care, and already lack access to affordable health care, this recommendation would further compound this problem. PCAs may provide health care services as a part of their job duties. Yet, they themselves are largely denied access.

DSPAM does support the governor's recommendation requiring PCA staff to be trained on: working with people with disabilities, infection control, mandated reporting, role of the PCA, basic transfers/lifting, changes in condition and HIPAA.

DSPAM supports requiring standardized trainings for agency owners and PCA staff. But, DSPAM does not support additional training requirements without increases in wages. Requiring additional training could decrease competitiveness of PCA wages when the majority of DSPs do not earn a livable wage.

The proposed budget changes to Personal Care Assistant Services will take money away from PCA wages, and this is an unacceptable solution to balancing the budget.

Thank you for the privilege of offering my testimony.

"Thank you," the chair of the committee said as she straightened her papers. She was a senator who was known for being supportive of the disability community.

Now I had a platform to address all the issues I had faced as a caregiver, along with tens of thousands in Minnesota and tens of millions across the country. I was no longer relegated to the dark corners of our communities. Instead, I was talking to lawmakers with a microphone—speaking out about the system I knew so well: the good, the bad, and a whole lot of ugly. With a larger vantage point, I saw myself objectively and realized that I was a small player in a massive system and I didn't deserve the conditions I had faced. This was my chance to do something about it, and I fiercely rose to the occasion. Serving others may have been what I was born into and work I fell into because it was familiar, but when I moved into advocacy, I realized that it was a calling and my passion for human rights was at the core of my commitment. I didn't believe in God anymore, but I did believe in justice.

Chapter 44: Scene One, Take...

It was surgery day again—the fourth surgery. Imani was thirteen years old. While she was growing, her bones continued to twist and rotate inward and had to be corrected repeatedly to avoid long-term issues from lack of alignment and improper posture.

Parking in the hospital ramp was limited. One of these days I would have to get around to getting a disability parking tag so we could park closer. Part of me felt that we should not take a spot that someone else might need more. Besides, I still expected that she would improve and not need accommodations—that the surgeries would reverse the CP, since it wasn't a "neurologically degenerative" condition. And when she was done growing, perhaps the surgeries would no longer be necessary. It was hard to accept help because sometimes other parents and advocates made comments that she "wasn't that disabled." But they didn't know what she had to deal with.

Both of Imani's femurs had to be derotated again and now her tibia, too. Plus, she was having her knee cap moved down and getting some ankle reconstruction. I gave Imani braids because she would be on bed rest for weeks and it would be hard to maintain her hair. Within days, it would be matted up like a bird's nest. A week in the hospital was kind of like dog years—a day felt more like seven. The requisite one-year recoveries seemed never-ending.

Imani got changed into a hospital gown, and I helped her settle into a bed with something to watch on TV. Family trickled in: my parents and then Imani's dad with his pregnant girlfriend.

Different medical professionals came in to collect information. Nurses took her vital signs and looked at her pre-op paperwork. The anesthesiologist explained the sedation process. Finally, Dr. Welling, the orthopedic surgeon, appeared through the curtain, already dressed in scrubs. He was calm and smiled warmly at Imani.

"I see you brought your crew with you," he joked and shook her hand, and then mine, and said hello to everyone else.

"They're actually just paid actors," Imani quipped. "I need to look important, you know."

Dr. Welling chuckled. "You rounded up a fine-looking group. Are they all staying?"

"Yep," she said. "Until you put my legs back on. Then we're going to have a dance party because you didn't make it to my last one. Not cool at all, Doc."

Everyone laughed and remarked how great she was doing. "She has always been a character," my mom told Dr. Welling.

"So, I'm going to draw on your legs with a marker where we're going to operate," Dr. Welling said as he took the cap off of a marker.

He marked up her legs and Imani made funny faces. "I'm not here for surgery; I'm getting tattoos! I want a pirate, too."

Dr. Welling laughed. "Did one of my nurses already give you some medicine?"

"Yeah, I drank the Kool-Aid!" She giggled.

"Where does she come up with this stuff?" my mom said, amused.

Then Dr. Welling left, and we waited for a nurse to come in with anti-anxiety medication to help Imani relax before surgery. Soon, she became quieter, with only the occasional silly comment or giggle. A nurse gave me scrubs to put on so I could go into the operating room with her, and I let the face mask rest below my chin. With the scrubs on, the seriousness of this event took hold and my mood changed instantly to anxious and frightened. I quit talking because I didn't want to start crying in front of Imani.

"Mom," Imani said with a look of playful sarcasm and tender appreciation, "you look beautiful, and it's not the drugs talking."

"Aw, thank you, Maners," I said, using one of her nicknames as I danced in a circle. "You don't think my scrubs make me look fat?"

"You're faaabulous, dahling," she drawled.

"Except for one thing…" She paused. "You need to turn that frown upside down. I'll just be gone for a little bit."

I looked at her, unsure how to respond. The words were reassuring, but the fact that my little girl was the one saying them made my heart feel like someone was wringing it out like a dish rag.

Mustering up courage to match hers, I said, "Then don't be gone long because you can't keep your mother waiting." As if on cue, Dr. Welling came back to say that it was time to go to the operating room. All I had left were a few more minutes of composure in me.

My mom took my things to bring to the waiting area, and I left with Imani and the nurses, who pushed her bed on wheels down the hall.

In the operating room, there was another bed waiting to transfer onto. A nurse at her head and a nurse at her feet, they slid her across to the bed where she would have surgery, encircled by machines.

Imani's face shifted from jovial to slightly terrified and she raised her eyebrows with big eyes as she looked at me as if to say that she was second-guessing the surgery. I hugged her, cheek to cheek, and put my hand on hers.

When the face mask was put on her face, she panicked, eyes darting all over. Instinctively, fighting back tears, I said as I had years ago in the NICU, "I love you, Imani. I'm so proud of you, sweetie," as her hand clenching mine went limp and her eyelids closed.

As soon as she was out, and not a second later, I wept out all the feelings: the sadness that my girl was going through this major surgery, the guilt that I as her mother couldn't prevent it, the anxiety around the procedure itself and whether she would be OK, the fear that she would be in pain, and the regret that she was spending her short childhood years going through surgeries and rehab and her summers in bed. It got harder with each surgery and year-long recovery. It was exhausting in every way and financially destructive.

I cried so much I couldn't talk as a nurse led me to the waiting area where my family and Marcus were and plopped into a chair as I continued to cry and wipe my eyes. "Ah, honey," my mom said as she rubbed my back. Everyone else was engaged in conversation. In the corner were two women talking quietly, and on the other side of the room were a mother and father who were on their cell phones. On the monitor, we could see the progress of the patients in surgery on a chart with a check mark in the box indicating their stage, under their initials. Imani was still being prepped. I felt like she was alone—the same way she seemed to be alone in the NICU. All I could do was be on the sidelines for her.

My mom rejoined the conversation that had turned to what we could do for fun this summer with Imani while she was recovering. "I was thinking that we could go to the zoo and see the dolphin show," she said.

"I seen that last summer," Marcus said. "She would like it, but her cast could get wet from all the splashing."

"Oh, right," mom replied. "They also do the bird show."

Marcus listed a lot of things that he thought would be good activities someone could do while in a wheelchair. It was annoying that he had swooped in like Superman to the rescue for this surgery when he never saw her and every time he called it was a fight. I didn't look at him while he rambled on and instead rolled my eyes at one of the women who was sitting in the corner, motioning toward Marcus. She looked at me empathetically. "Summer is fun if you can manage," she said. Her hair was dark blonde with an 80s perm and she wore medium-sized silver oval glasses. Frosted blue jeans hugged her overweight figure and she had on a baggy Nike "Just Do It" T-shirt.

"Lots of ideas to keep mom extra busy!" I said sarcastically, my voice shrill. My mom looked at me sympathetically and asked Marcus to go to the cafeteria with her.

The woman nodded and said, "When my son AJ was little, I was a single mom and I always wanted to do more with him than I could."

"AJ? I knew an AJ," I said. "That was the boyfriend of my friend, Jessica."

"No way! That's my AJ!" she said, shocked, leaning forward in her chair with her hands on her knees.

Stunned, I studied her face, but she wasn't familiar. "Oh my God, this is unbelievable. What are the odds that we would meet like this?" I mused. "You know that Jessica died, right?" I asked.

"Yes, AJ kept in touch with her. My name's Susan, by the way. Do you know what happened?" she asked.

I said that I didn't—that I had seen the obituary in the Star Tribune.

"It was suicide. She shot herself in the head when she was staying at her dad's house—why she was there with all he had done to her was a mystery. For the past few years, she had been living in group homes because she was schizophrenic and depressed. I'm assuming you didn't know any of this."

Her words sounded far away and seemed to echo as she told me the whole story of Jessica's death. I remembered back to a time that I had driven Jessica and Valerie to a park at sunset because Jessica insisted that she had to meet AJ there for their wedding.

When we arrived, Jessica pointed to a nondescript wooded area and whispered, "AJ is waiting here to marry me." Valerie told her that she was imagining things and, with an exasperated tone, told her that we needed to get home and she could call AJ later. Jessica laughed and put her hand on Valerie's arm, telling her that she could be her maid of honor. There was no AJ or a priest anywhere we looked.

"So that's what happened. Such a beautiful young woman, but so sick. You couldn't see it by looking at her. AJ was heartbroken, but now he has a girlfriend and she's having a baby. I'm going to be a grandma. Thought it would be AJ

and Jessica ending up together and making pretty bab
hard to know how life will turn out."

"Yeah," I said.

I told Susan the story of Jessica and me—that she was one of the only people there for me when I was pregnant and after my daughter was born. In fact, she was there for me through everything—from soon after Uncle Harold had raped me and throughout the time that I didn't know if he was the father until the paternity test, throughout Marcus' violent, explosive rages until we had a court order, and every day when Imani was in the NICU. Feeling vulnerable with my child under the knife, I was able to access my sorrow over losing Jessica and let out all of my other sorrows. There hadn't been time or mental space to process my grief.

Susan said that it wasn't my fault that men had abused me and that I should never feel guilty for other people's sins. Victims are not at fault, and it doesn't matter if you looked sexy or drank too much or found yourself in a vulnerable situation. There was no excuse for someone to violate you. Power imbalances also matter—like age differences, family relationships, and authority or money or some other economic advantage—it was complicated. Abusers are master manipulators who gaslight everyone into not seeing through their games, and they target people they think will be easy to dominate and silence.

Susan reinforced what I knew about the mentality of abusers and the dynamics of abuse and assaults, and I had to wonder how she knew so much. She made me feel less screwed up, confused, and ashamed. Although I knew a lot about my trauma intellectually, my pain still ran very deep.

"I don't know if anything happens for a reason," Susan said. "But sometimes we get our answers when we least expect it. Your answer is that little girl you are waiting here for."

"You are wonderful," I said. "I don't know how to thank you for this. But thank you. You're going to be a great grandma."

Susan smiled at me with a little wink and got up to get a cup of coffee. The monitor showed that Imani was already halfway through her surgery. Right then, the buzzer went off again and I called the OR for an update. She was doing great. They would call again when they were finishing up. I got up to get a cup of coffee, too. When I turned around, Susan was gone.

Sitting down, I looked at where she had been sitting and asked myself if my conversation with her had really taken place or was an illusion. My mom and Marcus came back from the cafeteria with some food for me.

"Here you go, sweetie," Mom said, handing me a tray with a grilled chicken sandwich and fries.

As I ate my lunch, Marcus talked with self-importance about the little he knew about Imani, like he saw her every day—weaving shreds of memories together to fabricate an impression that he was present in her life. By the way he laughed nervously, I knew that he realized that he hadn't even convinced himself.

His grandiosity grated on my last nerve. I was over his bullshit and all that was left of a deep love I once had for him was disgust. His charades were ridiculous, and he was pathetic. There was nothing else I had to say or wanted to hear.

The nurse came in to let us know that the surgery had gone well, and I exhaled—letting go of what Marcus thought anymore and relieved that the surgery was over. It was "Time to Move On," like the Tom Petty song.

A few weeks later, I got a bill in the mail for $20,000 for the surgery. Since I made just enough money for us not to qualify for State healthcare, we were on very expensive private insurance. The insurance company stated that they would pay for the surgery, but not the room and board—as if you go to a hospital for the hell of it. I fought the insurance company and got it reduced to $3,000 and got a payment plan that I still couldn't afford.

Chapter 45: Hear Me!

Every legislative session, the disability community holds a rally in the rotunda of the State Capitol in Saint Paul, Minnesota. Large groups of people pour out of buses, and smaller groups and individuals make their way from street parking and ramps surrounding the Capitol area. Today, I was giving a rally speech to advocate for the Personal Care Assistance (PCA) Services Program and a cost-of-living adjustment (COLA) to increase wages.

Good afternoon! Thank you for taking the time to come to YOUR Capitol today!

My name is Bridget Siljander, and I am here with the Direct Support Professional Association of Minnesota, also known as DSPAM.

We advocate for PCAs and other direct support professionals.

I have been a PCA since 1997 and have a daughter in high school, who has CP.

As many of us already know, PCAs are critical to the independence of people with disabilities. And we need to have a voice! Am I right?

That is why we have DSPAM—a voice for DSPs. We work in collaboration with other organizations like the sponsors of this great event today, to advocate for strengthening this very necessary workforce. And the RIGHTS of people with disabilities! This is about EQUALITY today!

We are here standing up for our rights and the support that we need from our community.

Are WE going to be heard today? Not tomorrow, TODAY? Are we going to be heard today?

This moment matters!

Let's educate our decision makers, so they can be informed and do the best by ALL of their constituents.

One thing we need is a RAISE, a RAISE for PCAs! And other direct support professionals!

(chant) A RAISE FOR PCAs!

We can't do our jobs very well when we are not supported! It is time for a COLA! We are asking TODAY for a COLA!

(Chant) COLA!!

We can't keep waiting on the basic supports we need! So, let's be heard today. Let's talk to our legislators today, and regularly. Build that relationship so they know that your needs matter. You are a Minnesotan and you have a voice!

Have a great day at YOUR Capitol!"

Pumping up the crowd was like lighting a wildfire—terrifying, contagious, glorious, and somewhat unexpected, but unstoppable and powerful. Nothing could extinguish us if we kept it going—lighting more and more of us... and fanning the flames of a people who had woken up.

Chapter 46: Ms. Education

Our city's fireworks are held within a day or so of the Fourth of July, and about 10,000 people attend. To get a decent viewing spot, it's advantageous to arrive hours before they begin. Since we're on Siljander time, we had to park about a mile away, and I had to carry our bag, with full water bottles.

As we settled in on a hill, after deliberating which spot was best, we checked our phones, read books on Kindle, and texted and Snapchatted family. I was reading Rachel Simon's *The Story of Beautiful Girl*. Imani had read it before me and was now reading *Once And For All* by Sarah Dessen.

Imani texted me: "I'm jealous of that girl eating cake."

I texted her back: "Her cake fell in the grass."

She showed me how much shorter her right leg (the "diva leg") still was than her left. I pointed out her different scars and said, "Dun, dun, dun, you could make a cool tattoo with them."

Laughing, she said, "I could have a tree on this leg and birds on the other," pointing to smaller scars on her left leg. "I actually want a tattoo, but I don't know what I'd get," I said, twisting my nose ring.

We listened to the Minnesota Orchestra as we waited for fireworks and the uncertain arrival of family. My sister texted me that she was just getting out of the shower, and I responded, "I think you're going to miss this one, punk." Nonetheless, I told everyone where we were sitting.

Imani said, "We need a bat signal that we can shine up that says 'Siljander.'" We were surrounded by masses of people:

some having picnics and drinking wine, a few with dogs, lots of kids and strollers, most people clearly more organized than us with amenities they had brought with them.

When the fireworks started, a lot of us stretched out on the grass to watch. As patriotic music played, the crowd gasped in amazement. The finale was worth everything with spectacularly bright pops of fireworks in a variety of colors and configurations.

I thought about how I had missed way too many moments like these with my daughter because I had such a large workload with my clients and school, plus compensating for what Marcus should have been helping with.

On the way home, Imani sang the song "Amore" to me. Then she unplugged my phone from the car charger and plugged hers in. Dean Martin sang "Amore" to us, and she said, "Sing it, Dean-O!" After singing along, and playing Andy Williams and Frank Sinatra, she remarked, "Imagine if these men had never gone to the studio. The world would be less bright—ahhhhh!" She loved old music and movies. Charles had introduced her to a lot of it. Somehow, the conversation turned to pancakes.

Imani said, "I need pancakes in my life."

"We have a mix, but it's easy to make pancakes from scratch, and they're better," I replied.

"Ooh! Let's get the ingredients this weekend!" she squealed.

I laughed. "You got it, kiddo!"

* * *

It was a brisk, bright fall day, and Imani was recovering from reconstructive hip surgery in our apartment. To pay for our rent, I had three jobs: employment consultant for Autism Works, direct support professional for Cubby, and waitress at a country club. Occasionally, if I still had steam left at the end of the day, I drove for Uber. A nonprofit I had started for disabled youth—The Youth Legacy Foundation—had to be sidelined while I kept the lights on in my own home. My sister Caitlin took care of Imani when I was at work, and I paid her using a chunk of Social Security back pay. Still, I had to stay within income and asset limits to protect her SSI. Imani was enrolled in the PSEO program that I had done, so she went to North Hennepin Community College instead of the last two years of high school. Charles drove Imani to some of her classes and occasionally took her out to dinner. He was still in her life as a chosen father, and they were close. I considered him one of my best friends.

"Imani, do you want to go out for a walk?" I asked. "It's not going to be this nice out for very much longer. AND I got you the Cadillac of crutch tips since the rubber is worn off of the one you have." Her pink forearm crutch, which she would eventually use again, was decorated with stickers and she referred to it as her "secret weapon." She was also going to get a wheelchair with a small motor ("power assist") for distance and energy conservation. It would be a good tool for getting around a bigger campus when she transferred to a four-year school. Her disability wasn't going away and it was an integrated part of her life, like my mental health was in mine. It took time to develop self-awareness and understanding of our experiences within the societal context as we gained more information—which was constantly changing with research, knowledge, advocacy, and greater awareness.

"Sure!" she said. We loved going on walks. It was a time to talk and laugh without distractions of homework and jobs and technology.

"Even after my long days, I have to come home and entertain your ass," I teased her.

"But I'm fun to hang out with," she quipped. "I'm like three glasses of wine."

Instantly, I belly laughed. "Yes, you are!"

She raised the head of her hospital bed (in the middle of our small living room) and wrapped her arms around my neck. I supported her like a sturdy oak tree as she turned to sit in her wheelchair.

"We look like two mysterious celebrities going around the block with our dark sunglasses on and my perennial head-to-toe all-black outfit. We're like The Addams Family," I said.

"I just need to have black hair in braids and be eating a cockroach," Imani said, not missing a beat, and I howled with laughter.

"No wonder nobody talks to us," I said. "We're two weirdos."

We talked about going to Europe and traveling by train. I said we needed to see the sights in Germany that Cubby had told me about, like the Hofbräuhaus in Munich. Imani pressed me to finally teach her German so we could speak it together.

A runner passed us by, raised his hand to Imani and said, "God bless you." Both of us looked at each other in disbelief, and then roared with laughter because it was so absurd, though not unusual for people to pity disability. We kept going, and he said it again on his way back.

"I think you should say something to him if he comes back," I told Imani. "He doesn't realize how condescending that is. First of all, how does he know if we even believe in God? And second of all, just don't, dude. We don't need your prayers; we're good."

Over the years, I had reconciled my spiritual convictions. God was a concept I didn't need. Love was the most reliable moral compass I had discovered, and it didn't divide people because it's universal. Compassion sustained me.

I saw no reason to attach myself to something that imprisoned me. But I understood why so many stayed in their religions and looked to religion for truth, predictability, community, strength, and purpose. And I could respect that. For many people, their faith is a core part of their identity and life and it compels them to do good and be kind. The church was like a dictator with rigid rules for conduct, and even thoughts, with a threat of punishment for not being perfect. My family had inherited this religious model without any agency to choose whether or not they wanted it. It didn't comfort them or provide guidance in the quest for truth or inspire universal love. Rather, it terrorized them into obedience.

I pointed out acerbically that we went further than usual today because, as Imani joked, he had blessed us twice.

When we got back to the apartment building, I checked the mailbox.

"Imani, you got something from the University of Minnesota!" I exclaimed.

She opened the envelope and read the letter:

Dear Imani,

Congratulations! We are pleased to inform you that your application for admission to the University of Minnesota College of Liberal Arts has been approved for Fall 2016.

We both shrieked and laughed, and I grabbed the letter from her to read it through myself.

"Imani, you can go to journalism school!" I almost yelled. She had been a teen cohost on the community television show Disability Viewpoints for several years and developed her advocacy through activities she did with me as well. "You are so ready for this! You can bring so much perspective and you got this, girl!"

That night for dinner, we had one of our favorites: macaroni and cheese. After that, it was time for more homework and I did my office work.

We worked more quickly and easily with a palpable sense of relief and energy. There was a shift; I could see the way forward—opening up beyond the next month or year—for Imani, and for me. If Imani lived on campus, both of us could be more independent, and I could regroup—rest after work, practice self-care, continue with trauma therapy, see friends, maybe even date... I knew now how to have a healthier relationship. I had quit smoking, cut back on drinking, and went for occasional walks now that I didn't need someone to stay with Imani. My mom took me to her gym with a guest pass and showed me how exercise can be a healthy stress reliever—now that I actually had a little time and bandwidth and the budget for a basic gym membership. But I was quite burned out and just wanted to sleep for a couple years first. Financials were unclear because I had no money, but we would try to figure it out like everything else with the help of the community.

I thought of Karen the nurse in those early days in the NICU while Imani's tiny body lay in an Isolette—her kind, compassionate, heartfelt words, her loving care, her nonjudgmental affirmations, and her big open spirit that filled up the place with a magic of peace and hope. I thought of Tricia, the social worker, who helped me find resources and financial assistance so our housing could stay secure and we had food to eat and a modicum of security from which to build a better life. The witches in my first apartment building who were new neighbors but loved me already and loved my baby they had never met. I thought of all the people I had worked with as a caregiver over the years and what they had taught me about living with disability and dealing with socioeconomic barriers. And Auntie Rose, whom I missed and loved so much and whose example showed me that life goes on one way or another. Mark taught me about reimagining your life after change and paying it forward through mentoring. He, Cubby and Joe had been my biggest cheerleaders, as I had been theirs. Their disabilities didn't go away—they were part of them—and they didn't get their old lives back, but life was still worth living. Their appreciation and validation of me warmed me and filled me with pride. The times I had shown up for them gave me a deep sense of satisfaction, and I looked back on my service like a true patriot. My family was still a family, despite the division along church lines. My parents had done their best with me, as I had with Imani. Mom told me that Imani looked right at her the first time she saw her, and she was instantly in love—and that my parents had visited her weekly in the hospital. I didn't remember that, but Mom did, and she also remembered how dazed and exhausted I was, but totally devoted to Imani. Through ongoing, sometimes intermittent, conversation with my family, we partially healed our imperfect relationships, heard each other's sides of the stories, and empathized with each other more. We mutually agreed to work it out during the times we engaged. Imani got to grow up knowing and enjoying them because these relationships were managed. I also explained the dynamics of the church to her to establish healthy boundaries and make it possible for her to be part of the bigger family and their community.

Bad things still happened, but the string of paper suns was always there, reminding me that there was good in the world, no matter what was happening, or what the church tried to tell us about "unbelievers." Their love showed me the way. They got me—US—through to a brighter day. They were speaking up, supporting others, activating, healing, and whatever they were able to do. And yet, they were fragile, too—vulnerable, afraid, lonely, lost. They didn't have everything, nor were they perfect or necessarily in the best position to offer much. Despite their own struggles and weaknesses, they cared about and connected with people around them and their communities. After a surgery during middle school, Imani had once said, "Beauty on the outside is art; beauty on the inside is a masterpiece."

"We are so lucky, Imani," I said. "And we are not less—or more—than anyone else."

Turning to me with a contemplative look of agreement, she said, "I know."

Afterword

It is now January 2019, and Imani and I have just spent the holidays in Europe, traveling through Germany and France. This was not our first time either; we took our first trip to Europe together in summer 2012 when we traveled through Germany and Austria. Both Imani and I speak German and enjoy studying foreign languages; it's one of our shared interests, along with reading, writing, music, and art. We are also both passionate about human rights.

I have continued with my work in activism, and in spring 2019, Imani is graduating from the University of Minnesota Hubbard School of Journalism and Mass Communication with a bachelor's degree in journalism and minor in history. She is an associate reporter for the *Minnesota Daily* newspaper at the University and cohost of the community television show *Disability Viewpoints*. Like me, she completed her general education at North Hennepin Community College. We love both schools and feel fortunate to have been given the opportunities to attend. Education has transformed our lives in many ways, opened up a wealth of possibilities for each of us, and primed us to be lifelong learners with deep curiosity about the world and its people and creatures.

Our lives have been educational experiences as well, which is why I have great appreciation for the value of lived experience, especially when it impacts decision making. Imani and I are longtime advocates on a variety of issues and have participated in many activities to help solve community problems and issues. We bring both our classroom and real-world education to our work and use our perspectives to broaden representation across platforms—her through journalism primarily and me through my nonprofit The Youth Legacy Foundation, other disability rights advocacy projects, and electoral politics. It is important for people with diverse experiences to participate in civic engagement and politics to promote inclusion. I think our backgrounds have expanded our thinking in such a way that we are able to be more mindful of inclusion of diversity overall.

Since the early years raising Imani, I have seen a lot of social and political change, improvements in attitudes, and improvements in the community at large, but many of the old problems remain, such as lack of equity and access to power, resources, and spaces. Caregivers—or direct support professionals—do not earn a living wage and account for millions of our working poor; disabled people/people with disabilities are marginalized, discriminated against, and forced into poverty; single mothers do not receive adequate support; inaccessible, unaffordable healthcare is causing people to go without basic care, lose everything, and even die; and violence against women and girls is still commonplace.

Through increased awareness, sometimes facilitated by social media, we as a collective are learning more about the realities that many people are living—people whose lives have historically been invisible. Activism has become mainstream. Information can be shared rapidly. There are many avenues and tools to address systemic oppression and build healthier communities. Our everyday lives are impacted by policies that are created and enforced. Our shared work continues to reimagine a world we want to live in and leave for our children, and when people come together and do what we are able to, we can accomplish a lot. Everything we do matters.

Last month, I took Imani to a new Hennepin County human services center ("hub"), which was much different from the one I wrote about in the chapter #3420. It was not cramped and depressing; rather it was bright and modern, more private, and the customer service was excellent. Regardless of political persuasion or opinions on socioeconomic issues, people who need help still deserve to be treated with dignity and respect. We can have different ideas of HOW we move our society forward, but it should never include dehumanizing people in the process. I spoke with one of the workers who shared some of the changes with me, such as people retiring (along with their outdated views on social systems), significantly more training, staff being better educated with bachelor's and master's degrees, more workers, less crowding, improved service coordination, accessible locations, and the transformations that have come with technological advances. Also, policy affects practice in government systems, so it depends on who is in a position of power, like the county commissioner. Learning about how our government and community entities are structured and operated helps to understand them from a bigger-picture perspective. In the chapter #3420, I wanted to show how the poor and struggling are treated not only by the systems, which are broken in many ways, but by society as a whole since our systems reflect our society. As we evolve, so too should our systems.

Storytelling is a major component of advocacy, and that was a major motivator for me to write *A String of Paper Suns*—to provide insight and promote compassion, and also to activate people to engage in their communities as they are able and their resources allow. We all have our own individual capacities, skills, gifts, talents, and situations. In a sense, this is a testimony. So, in conclusion, I would like to make a call to action and ask readers to think about what they can be or do to contribute. If you have access to the Internet, you can find many options. It could be a way to affect change around something you care about, whether it's calling a representative to tell your story or encourage them to vote a certain way, helping a single mother, being an ally or friend, donating to a group or an organization, volunteering for a cause or at an event, campaigning for a candidate, or writing a letter. And VOTE. There are websites you can go to for ways to get involved, and some organizations have such links on their websites. Advocacy can also be fun and a great way to meet people and feel more connected—growing your own string of paper suns. For me, it has given me purpose and a support system; you often do get more from it than you give. Plus, you can feel good about doing something instead of sitting with frustration about issues.

Being politically active has allowed me to observe social change up close and personal. Even though the larger issues may not shift dramatically or quickly, as they are often slow and challenging to address, you can gain an insider perspective of where movement is taking shape. There are many little victories on the path toward big victories. If we do what we can from where we are, we can change the world together.

Acknowledgments

The material in this book was derived from my observations and memories as well as in-depth research into the socioeconomic barriers faced by those impoverished and those with disabilities. I am deeply grateful to everyone in the community who has lifted me up during all of my adversities. I could not have completed this project without the warmth and insight from my beloved friends and supporters.

I am indebted to readers and supporters who have offered me encouragement and feedback to help make this book the best it can be and keep me going: Deb Holtz, Linda Erickson, Leah Smith, Kevin O'Brien, Amy Hewitt, Rielly Grey, Jim du Bois, Siobhan Kierans, Natasha Sporborg, Brad Gangnon, Yvette Hoffman, Kirk Johnson, Aisha Gomez, Angela Conley, Janet Morgan, Liesl Rohland, Cassandra Brandt, Julie Moulton, Alex Mattila, Rachael Sarto, Rodney Metzger, Linnea Hoff, Brigette Anderson, Caroline Joy Adams, Lisa Kidder, Jeanette Eastman, Julie Kenney, Kevin Murphy, Nathan Wornhoff, Joseph Crowe, Levette Brown, Kathryn Madson, Milpha Blamo, Tomika Nicole, Toni Jean Longo, Crystal Joy Hanson, Kavita Mehta, Gene Martinez, Ingrid Hofmann, Leila Hill, Tammy Rowe Wallace, Gayle Carlson, Lisa Salazar, Paul Oja, Michael Neuvirth, and Brad Copeland.

In addition, I am thankful to many advocates and friends in the disability community who have taught me and given me space to grow as a person and in my work.

Special thanks go to my family and people I have worked with as a direct support professional and advocate, who have courageously allowed me to tell our stories.

Sincere appreciation goes to Minneapolis City Council Member, Cameron Gordon, who suggested that I include people in the community who helped me when telling my story.

My lovely friend, Angela King-Jones, who generously gave me artistic direction and input during the book-cover-design process.

I am grateful to my copyeditor, Zora Knauf, for her engaging personality, immediate enthusiasm, and thoughtful dedication to my book. She is incredibly knowledgeable and was a rockstar to work with.

I am honored to have worked with Anne Dubuisson on book development. She brought the story out of me with her intuition and savvy and both inspired me throughout the challenging process of writing my complex story and provided me with a wealth of knowledge about the craft of writing.

My wonderful mentor and friend, Rachel Simon, has believed in me and my abilities since we met many years ago, and her generosity and expertise changed my life and brought my dream of writing my memoir to fruition.

One of the first and best people I met in my disability community work, Mike Patrick, whose belief in me during some of my darkest times enabled me to become part of something bigger than myself.

Deep appreciation to my dear friend and mentor, John Smith, who changed my life by introducing me to the world of disability rights advocacy and his dedication to the cause.

Immense gratitude to my perennial cheerleader, Jeff Reichel, who has been there for me since I met him as a 21-year-old single mom and was instrumental to my going back to college and forging a career. Without his enthusiasm and support, I would've been lost.

To my longtime friend, Gary Groomes, to whom I owe everything—including money. But honestly, he has been a wonderful substitute father to Imani and helpful to this process in countless ways.

I am especially grateful to my amazing daughter, Imani, who taught me what real love is.

I am blessed to know all of you.

About the Author

Bridget Siljander is a nationally known disability rights advocate and community organizer and the founding director of The Youth Legacy Foundation, an organization for disabled youth that expands access to community-based opportunities. She has written extensively on disability and other human rights issues.

Reading Group Guide: Discussion Questions

1. Which characters did you find relatable and why?
2. How did the author humanize each of the characters, and do you feel it helps understand them within a greater context?
3. How does a string of paper suns symbolize community?
4. Describe the impact of music on the empowerment of Bridget.
5. How do the italicized sections of the book, which relay Bridget's history, inform the chapters that take place during and after Imani's birth? How do these chapters serve to explain Bridget's character trajectory?
6. Discuss the evolution of Bridget's relationship with her family before and after Imani is born.
7. Reflect on the role of patriarchy (and its connection with the church) in Bridget and Imani's lives.
8. Explore the critique of religion in this book. Is it fair? How does it highlight differences in religious perspectives?
9. Why does Bridget struggle with self-determination and self-esteem? Why does she struggle to understand and enforce boundaries?
10. Is there justice in the story, and what does it look like?
11. Does the book make you think differently about parenthood and reproductive choice? How?
12. Discuss the representation of disability and how it evolves parallel to the growth of the characters.

13. Discuss the significance of mental health and how it is understood and responded to by the characters. Bridget? Jessica? Marcus? Charles? Others?
14. Discuss some of the impacts of labeling and treating people like they are special and how it can be detrimental. Some examples in the book: treating someone like they are special for being pretty or gifted academically, people being treated like they are special because they are part of a certain religion, and labeling people with disabilities as "special" or "special needs."
15. Discuss how equality and equity are not special treatment and what they actually look like.
16. What are examples of socioeconomic supports that empowered the characters? What seemed effective? Where should the community invest more supports and resources? How would this promote health, prosperity, and wellbeing?

Author Recommendations

Books

All the Weight of Our Dreams: On Living Racialized Autism by Autism Women's Network, Lydia X.Z. Brown (Editor), E. Ashkenazy (Editor)

Always Looking Up: The Adventures of an Incurable Optimist by Michael J. Fox

Beyond Belief: My Secret Life Inside Scientology and My Harrowing Escape by Jenna Miscavige Hill

Criminal of Poverty: Growing Up Homeless in America by Tiny aka Lisa Gray-Garcia

Designed by God, So I Must be Special by Bonnie Sose

An Examination of the Pearl by Edwin Suominen

Fading Scars: My Queer Disability History by Corbett Joan OToole

GIMP: When Life Deals You a Crappy Hand, You Can Fold – or You Can Play by Mark Zupan

Good Kings Bad Kings by Susan Nussbaum

I See Your Face Before Me: A Father's Promise by Murray B. Schneps

I Still Believe in Tomorrow by Mike Patrick

Leaving the Fold: A Guide for Former Fundamentalists and Others Leaving Their Religion by Marlene Winell, Ph.D.

Nerdy, Shy, and Socially Inappropriate: A User Guide to an Asperger Life by Cynthia Kim

Nobody Nowhere: The Extraordinary Autobiography of an Autistic Girl by Donna Williams

Nothing About Us Without Us: Disability Oppression and Empowerment by James I. Charlton
Oh, The Places You'll Go! by Dr. Seuss
Operating Instructions: A Journal of My Son's First Year by Anne Lamott
The Reason I Jump: The Inner Voice of a Thirteen-Year-Old Boy with Autism by Naoki Higashida, K.A. Yoshida (Translator), David Mitchell (Translator)
Riding the Bus with My Sister by Rachel Simon
The Heart's Alphabet: Daring to Live with Cerebral Palsy by James Grimm
The Story of Beautiful Girl by Rachel Simon
We Sinners by Hanna Pylväinen

Television Shows

Breaking Amish
Return to Amish
Teen Mom
Unexpected

A String of Paper Suns Playlist

This playlist includes songs that were mentioned in the book, songs that were meaningful to me throughout the timeline of this story, and songs that enliven the story and add another layer to its messages.

You can find the "A String of Paper Suns" playlist on Spotify by searching for "Bridget Siljander" or for the playlist itself.

"This Land Is Your Land" – Woody Guthrie
"Wildwood Flower" – The Carter Family
"Goober Peas" – P. Nutt
"It Ain't Gonna Rain No More" – Wendell Woods Hall
"This Old Man (Knick-Knack Patty-Whack)" – Unknown
"Take Me Out to the Ballgame" – Jack Norworth & Albert Von Tilzer
"Old Dan Tucker" – Dan Emmett
"It's a Small World" – Robert & Richard Sherman
"You Are My Sunshine" – Johnny Cash
"You Are My Sunshine" – Elizabeth Mitchell
"Like A Prayer" – Madonna
"Like A Virgin" – Madonna
"Papa Don't Preach" – Madonna
"Material Girl" – Madonna
"Unchained Melody" – The Righteous Brothers
"Wild World" – Cat Stevens
"Morning Has Broken – Cat Stevens
"Over The Rainbow" – Judy Garland

"Mary Jane's Last Dance" – Tom Petty and the Heartbreakers
"Free Fallin'" – Tom Petty
"Runnin' Down A Dream" – Tom Petty and the Heartbreakers
"All That She Wants" – Ace of Base
"Self Esteem" – The Offspring
"Come as You Are" – Nirvana
"Is There Life Out There" – Reba McEntire
"Wind of Change" – Scorpions
"Dance to the Music" – Sly & The Family Stone
"Everyday People" – Sly & The Family Stone
"Silent All These Years" – Tori Amos
"It's Oh So Quiet" – Björk
"Lose Yourself" – Eminem
"Rockin' in the Free World" – Neil Young
"Heart of Gold" – Neil Young
"Don't Let Go" – En Vogue
"Learning To Fly" – Tom Petty
"Doll Parts" – Hole
"Only God Knows Why" – Kid Rock
"Have You Ever Seen The Rain" – Creedence Clearwater Revival
"Summer of '69" – Bryan Adams
"21st Century (Digital Boy)" – Bad Religion
"Fuck Authority" – Pennywise
"Sheena is a Punk Rocker" – Ramones
"Bad Reputation" – Joan Jett & The Blackhearts
"Loser" – Beck
"Killing in the Name" – Rage Against the Machine
"Guerrilla Radio" – Rage Against the Machine

"Don't Bring Me Down" - Electric Light Orchestra
"Turn To Stone" - Electric Light Orchestra
"Family Affair" – Mary J. Blige
"Rhythm is a Dancer" – SNAP!
"What is Love" – Haddaway
"Another Night" – Real McCoy
"Only Happy When It Rains" – Garbage
"Mr. Vain" – Culture Beat
"Scatman" – Scatman John
"Where Do You Go" – No Mercy
"Blowin' In the Wind" – Bob Dylan
"Like a Rolling Stone" – Bob Dylan
"Tangled up in Blue" – Bob Dylan
"Violet" – Hole
"Live To Tell" – Madonna
"Wish You Were Here" – Pink Floyd
"Faded" – Alan Walker
"Old Man" – Neil Young
"Losing My Religion" – R.E.M.
"Everybody Hurts" – R.E.M.
"Dreams" – The Cranberries
"Zombie" – The Cranberries
"Hand In My Pocket" – Alanis Morissette
"Bullet With Butterfly Wings" – The Smashing Pumpkins
"Toxic" – Britney Spears
"These Boots Are Made For Walkin'" – Nancy Sinatra
"Shimmy Shimmy Ko-Ko-Bop" – Little Anthony & The Imperials
"You Belong To Me" – The Duprees
"My Eyes Adored You - Frankie Valli
"Rocking Around the Christmas Tree" – Johnny Marks

"Born This Way" – Lady Gaga
"Fancy" – Reba McEntire
"A Mighty Fortress Is Our God" – Martin Luther
"Children of the Heavenly Father" – Lina Sandell-Berg
"What A Wonderful World" – Louis Armstrong
"We Are The World" – Michael Jackson
"Fight the Power" – Public Enemy
"Testify" – Rage Against the Machine
"Time To Move On" – Tom Petty
"That's Amore" – Dean Martin
"One Love" – Bob Marley
"People Got To Be Free" – The Rascals
"Come Together" – The Beatles
"Imagine" – John Lennon
"People Have The Power" – Patti Smith

Resources

There are many organizations on the national, state, and regional levels where you can learn more about disability, advocacy, anti-poverty and intersectional work, and other social issues addressed in this book and get involved. Here are some I recommend. Many of them also have a social media presence and resources on their websites.

Access Press
www.accesspress.org

ADA Information Line
www.ada.gov/infoline.htm

ADAPT
adapt.org

Advocating Change Together (ACT)
www.selfadvocacy.org

American Association on Intellectual and Developmental Disabilities (AAIDD)
www.aaidd.org

American Network of Community Options and Resources (ANCOR)
www.ancor.org

The Arc
www.thearc.org

The Arc Minnesota
www.arcminnesota.org

Association of University Centers on Disabilities (AUCD)
www.aucd.org

Autism Society
www.autism-society.org

Autism Society of Minnesota
ausm.org

Autistic Self Advocacy Network (ASAN)
autisticadvocacy.org

Black Women's Blueprint
www.blackwomensblueprint.org

Courage Center
www.allinahealth.org/Courage-Kenny-Rehabilitation-Institute/

DirectCourse
directcourseonline.com

Disability Hub MN
disabilityhubmn.org

Gender Justice
www.genderjustice.us

Institute on Community Integration (ICI)
www.ici.umn.edu

Interact
interactcenter.org

Jeremiah Program
www.jeremiahprogram.org

KFAI
kfai.org

LiveOn
liveon.net

Metro Mobility
www.metrotransit.org/metro-mobility

Metropolitan Center for Independent Living (MCIL)
www.mcil-mn.org

Minnesota Coalition Against Sexual Assault
www.mncasa.org

NARAL Pro-Choice America
www.prochoiceamerica.org

The National Alliance for Direct Support Professionals (NADSP)
www.nadsp.org

The National Alliance on Mental Illness (NAMI)
www.nami.org

National Council on Independent Living (NCIL)
www.ncil.org

OutFront Minnesota
www.outfront.org

PACER
www.pacer.org

Planned Parenthood
www.plannedparenthood.org

Rape, Abuse & Incest National Network (RAINN)
www.rainn.org

Self-Advocates Becoming Empowered (SABE)
www.sabeusa.org

The Youth Legacy Foundation (YLF)
www.youthlegacyfoundation.org